CROSSROADS
Approaches in Modern Studies

INDUSTRIAL CHANGE
cause and consequence

Roderick Stuart

Modern Studies Teacher
Cranhill Secondary School
Glasgow

Blackie

CROSSROADS

GENERAL EDITORS:

Ian Graham
Adviser in Social Subjects

Alex Stirling
Adviser in Modern Studies

ISBN   0 216 90366 1

PUBLISHED BY:
Blackie & Son Limited
Bishopbriggs, Glasgow G64 2NZ
450 Edgware Road, London W2 1EG

PRINTED IN GREAT BRITAIN BY:
Robert MacLehose & Company Limited
Printers to the University of Glasgow

Preface

CROSSROADS aims to provide a basis for the examination and further study of the underlying and developing influences which affect contemporary institutions, issues and affairs.

The series is designed to meet the needs of school pupils and students in Further Education who are undertaking a course in Modern Studies at the S.C.E. Higher Grade. The texts also will be found useful for those following courses in General Studies for G.C.E.

The subjects covered include industrial organization and development, social change, political parties in Great Britain, race relations, the Great Powers and international relations.

Ian Graham
Alex Stirling

Acknowledgments

The author and publisher would like to thank the following for permission to reproduce copyright material.

The Guardian: page (vi)
Northern Industrial Photographers Ltd: page (vi)
National Coal Board: pages 3, 12, 13, 16, 18
The British Petroleum Co. Ltd: page 5
Chrysler Scotland Ltd: page 27
British Leyland U.K. Ltd: page 42
Hughes Microelectronics Ltd: page 43
Aerofilms Ltd: page 45
George Hodge Associates: page 51
Central Office of Information: page 68

Contents

Workington in outline: pithead and steel plant—two great staple industries of the last century.

The modern working environment—I.C.I.'s Hexagon Tower in Manchester houses technical services for the fast-growing organic chemicals industry.

Old and New

THE OLD...

It all began calmly enough in 1951. That year, in the bible-thick, gold-embossed county development plan, amid the maps of ancient monuments and the diagrams of sewerage systems, appeared this statement: 'Many of the rows of houses which grew up around the pitheads have outlived their usefulness and, as the uneconomic pits close and coal working is concentrated in more economic workings, a gradual regrouping of population should take place. Indeed the very reason for the existence of some of these small isolated places will disappear completely and new development and redevelopment in some of the better placed settlements will not only be better adjusted to the future pattern of employment opportunity but will also offer better living conditions than ever before to many of the inhabitants of the county.'

With the 'cold facts' of this general policy there were at first few quarrels. At the first public enquiry on the plan in 1952, only 2 of the county's 31 district councils objected. What was later to arouse increasing resistance, when put into practice, was the plan's rigid division of Durham's 357 towns and villages into four categories which would rule future capital investment.

In 70 category-A places, with a predicted population growth resulting in large part from the regrouping of settlements policy, there would be substantial further investment. In 143 B places there would be sufficient capital injection to cater for an anticipated static population. In 30 C places, a minimum

1

investment to meet the needs of an expected slowly declining population.

There has been little difficulty about these ABCs. The difficulties and the dissensions have resulted from the 114 category-D places (since increased by seven villages), defined in the plan as 'those from which a considerable loss of population may be expected. In these cases it is felt that there should be no further investment of capital on any considerable scale.'[1]

Changes in industrial activity, affecting the coal and steel industry in particular, are leading to the slow death of 121 village communities.

It has brought about an almost total ban on any new housing, public or private, in the D settlements, which are dejected places with inappropriate names like Eden Pit, Sunniside and Mount Pleasant or with appropriate names like Burnt Houses, The Slack and Pity Me. There the D label has come to mean derelict, doomed, damned.[1]

The background against which Durham County Council made this harsh decision in 1951 was a drop of 65,000 colliery jobs in the preceding 25 years and a need to attract no less than 97,000 new jobs before 1961 just to maintain existing population and its natural increase.

They faced a steady loss of people, especially the young and the skilled, through emigration from the county. Declining numbers resulted in declining social facilities, such as cinemas, social clubs and the like. A quarter of a century later, these problems still confront the reformed Durham County Council, and the people who elect them.

Witton Park (a D-category village) had a 5000 population in 1950, down to 2000 today. It is a place where, says Alan York, a local councillor, 'there used to be dances, a boys' club, everything you'd want. Now it's all drifting away, we're dying a slow death.'[1]

Then as now the drop in rateable value, one of the inevitable results of falling population, puts a strain on the provision of public services, which is hardly helped by the tendency for the population to 'cluster' into two 'expensive' categories: the very *young* and

Coal in decline: from more than a million to less than a quarter of a million men in 50 years.

the very *old*. Education for the young and health and welfare for the old and young has to be provided by a community whose earning power is being steadily reduced.

Failure to attract the extra jobs they projected in 1951, made worse by the continued and even more rapid decline in employment in the pits—100,000 miners worked the Durham coalfield in 1960; by 1973, only 28,000 remained—has had the inevitable, dismal results.

This single, local example, which could so easily be repeated throughout the north of England, Wales, Scotland or Northern Ireland, shows that the decline of an old industry is not a matter merely of complex theories. It has a pervasive, dramatic effect on the lives of ordinary people. And it does not affect only their working lives, as the example of Witton Park shows. Social life, family life and the morale of the community all suffer.

AND THE NEW

East Kilbride is Scotland's first new town. Designated in 1947, it has grown from a population of 2500 in 1950, when the first new houses were completed, to 53,000 in 1967. In that period 14,000 houses, 120 factories (nearly 4 million square feet),

3

141 shops (291,500 square feet), 14 schools (12,000 places), and 11 churches have been built. The Development Corporation will continue to promote the rapid growth of the town by attracting new industry and people until the population is 70,000. Thereafter, it will grow naturally to about 100,000 becoming one of the biggest towns in Scotland.

East Kilbride is a happy and prosperous town. The citizens are warm in their appreciation of their good houses and environment. Children are clean, healthy and vigorous. There is no unemployment problem. Paradoxically, the labour supply is plentiful; only by getting a job in the town can people qualify for a house—and the demand for housing is insatiable. Industrial relations are excellent. The standard of labour is high—only 11 per cent of the working population is unskilled. Workers and wives want new furnishings and equipment for their new house, a motor car and all the good things of life. They work hard to earn them.[2]

Allowing for the public relations 'gloss' that such a publicity document assumes—clean children indeed!—it is still clear that this situation is one far removed from that of the Durham pit villages.

It conforms to the simple pattern: old industries = bad; new industries = good. The reality, of course, is not so clear cut. The arrival of new industries in an area may cause considerable upheaval. Although its arrival may be welcomed by the local people, a new industry brings problems of adjustment also.

Just such a situation is the arrival of the oil industry in the north-east of Scotland. This area was well used to losing population through lack of jobs locally. Outside the only large town (Aberdeen), the principal industry was farming, and the numbers required in that, and related servicing and manufacturing industries, had been steadily declining over the years.

Exploration for oil in the North Sea off the coast of this relatively poor region of Scotland, itself a relatively poor part of the United Kingdom, must seem like the arrival of an industrial fairy godmother. But,

ask someone in or around Aberdeen what difference oil has made to his life, and the most likely answer will be that he can't get anyone to do his house repairs.[3]

4

B.P.'s North Sea oil drilling rig Sea Quest: *hope for the future; source of jobs; provider of energy; supplier of materials for industry—and wrecker of communities?*

This is a small matter to those who devise economic policy for an advanced industrial country, but no small matter to someone with a leaking water pipe. It colours his perception of 'progress'.

Oil-related developments are land-hungry. This is how one local community newspaper, *Aberdeen Peoples Press*, saw the impact of oil on the city:

> Apart from losing Old Torry, we are also losing other amenities such as the three cinemas in the city centre which are being 'redeveloped' to meet the most pressing of community needs —office accommodation.[3]

To the people of Witton Park in Durham, the arrival of new oil-related industries would appear as a godsend. To the inhabitants of the town of Peterhead in the north-east of Scotland, it is not so clearly a salvation.

As coal was the basis of life in the Durham pit villages, so herring was crucial to Peterhead. The herring fishing has virtually disappeared. But it is at the heart of the 'off-shore supply' industry that has grown in the early 1970s. The result is that the Peterhead employment exchange area had the lowest rate of unemployment in Britain at the end of 1974. In this and in other oil-boom areas, however, all is not seen as 'sweetness and light'.

Some of the local senior citizens painted a more sober picture of the oil-boom town. In a variety of ways, the community was suffering and the environment was being spoiled; the drainage difficulties would make sewage a curse along the coast. Peterhead was losing the people a community needed: its clerks were going to the Aberdeen offices, scarcely a baker was left in the town, the carpenters and engineers were being grabbed by the big firms. It was difficult to recruit teachers to the district, which had never produced enough of its own: if a young primary teacher earned less than £30 a week, she couldn't compete for lodgings with construction crews earning up to £100.

One farmer I spoke to could not get the labour for much-needed modernization of his farm.[3]

Further north, the small town of Cromarty looks across the Cromarty Firth to the giant crane of Highland Fabricators Ltd at Nigg, used in the manufacture of oil production platforms.

At nights the arc lights in Nigg glare brilliantly across the water at Cromarty, where the shadows lie darkly. The Hi-Fab construction site at Nigg is to be doubled in size, and now Cromarty Petroleum hope to build a refinery there, the first in the north of Scotland.

But now Cromarty is liable to lose its tourist attraction, and yet not have the resources or resilience either to gain genuine long-term profit from the huge growth across the water or effectively to resist whatever pollution may fall out from the proposed refinery.[3]

These doubts from the 'boom' areas of Aberdeen, Peterhead and the Cromarty Firth surely point out the inapplicability of any simple equation between the arrival of new industry and a 'happy ever after' outcome.

CHANGE FOR THE BETTER?

If industrial change brings material benefits, it brings human disruption also. The loss of an old industry must affect the life of any community. At its worst, the community will lingeringly wither and die, as with so many of Durham's pit villages.

In this more mobile age a small community which loses its independent economic existence may become a satellite of some larger centre nearby. This turns a once thriving community into a dormitory for those who spend most of their active lives elsewhere. This has been the case with many East Anglian villages where falling labour requirements have meant the decline of rural economic opportunities. Such a case is Ronald Blythe's *Akenfield*.

> The young men are beginning to realize that the farming scene has no future for them unless they happen to be farmers' sons and can inherit. The middle-aged workers bore them with their tales of thirty-bob-a-week-and-all-hours but the more intelligent teenager has already discovered that his farming life must in essence be his father's farming life repeated— plus sufficient training to allow him to cope with the new agricultural machinery.[4]

The result of this is that many young people leave. The 1961 Census population of 'Akenfield' was 298, compared to the 1931 figure of 416. The only chance for survival of the community, albeit in a form quite transformed, lies in the attraction of the 'new commuters'.

The arrival of a new industry, especially where it brings new people, will also cause changes in the familiar patterns of life. Such a threat from the oil industry impelled the islanders of the Shetlands to seek legal powers to control the impact of the new industry on their proudly independent, on-going life style.

The building of new communities in existing industrial areas to act as focal or growth points for the establishment of new industries has been severely called into question. The time lapse between the building of a 'bricks and mortar' town and the growth of a community has caused genuine unhappiness to many early residents. The limited attractions for industrial firms of these modern creations; the immense cost of building on virgin sites; the unbalanced population that the new towns recruit; the undemocratic form of their government; opposition from older towns to the disproportionate share of job opportunities going to the new towns—all these drove the House of Commons Expenditure

7

Committee, in their Thirteenth Report (October 1975), to question the validity of this form of regional development.

This is not a marginal aspect of British life. Industrial change is endemic. It affects both the individual and the community. Changes in the distribution of job opportunities between different industries is marked, even over a short period of time. During the working life of one miner, employment in the coal industry has fallen from well over a million at the time of the 1926 General Strike to less than a quarter of that number. In the last twenty years alone, there has been a decline from nearly 800,000 to 240,000.

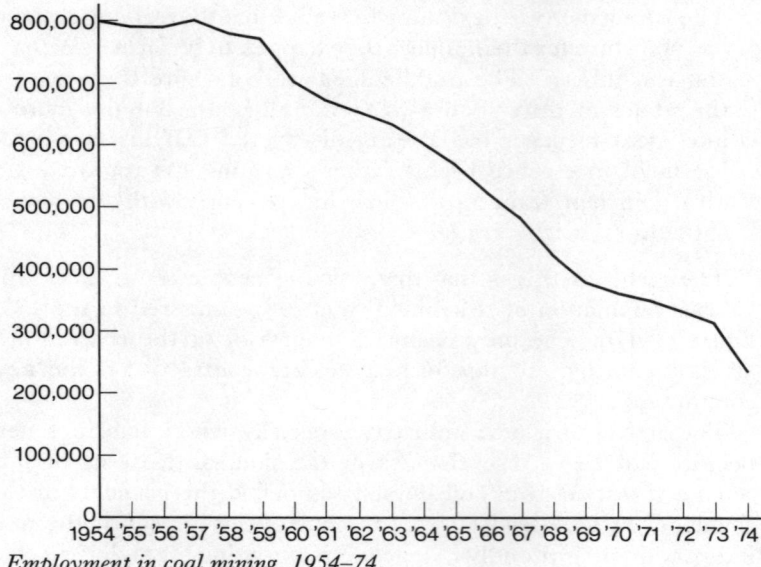

Employment in coal mining, 1954–74.

At the same time, new industries have grown from small beginnings. In 1926, I.C.I. was formed from four companies involved mainly in general chemicals, dye-stuffs and explosives. That giant is now the leader in an industry which produces a vast range of synthetic substitutes, plastics, paint, fertiliser and other chemical compounds which either did not exist or were at the experimental stage 50 years ago. The motor vehicle and aircraft industries have grown beyond the recognition of an observer of the 1920s. Electronics is only now beginning to realize its colossal potential.

Table 1.1 shows the proportions of the work-force in 1921 and in 1971 engaged in twelve major industries. It reveals the extent of the transformation in the distribution of job opportunities between industries during the working lifetime of one person.

Industry	1921	1971
Farming	6·6	1·8
Coal mining	6·6	1·6
Iron and steel	1·3	1·2
Shipbuilding and marine engineering	2·1	0·9
Textiles	6·6	2·8
Chemicals	1·1	2·0
Electrical engineering	0·9	3·7
Motor vehicles	1·5	2·3
Retail trade	6·9	8·2
Insurance, banking, finance and business services	1·3*	4·4
Educational services	2·0*	6·8
Medical and dental services	0·8*	4·8

* 1921 figures are estimates: grouping of trades was different in 1921 from that in 1971; if anything, they are underestimates

Table 1.1   *The percentage of the industrial work force employed in twelve industries, 1921 and 1971*

Since this trend is far from diminishing, it is clear that our working lives are going to involve constant re-adjustment to changes in employment. We need to understand what brings about a change in the number of jobs available in any trade or industry.

[1] 'Durham's Murdered Villages' by John Barr   (NEW SOCIETY 3 April 1969)
[2] *East Kilbride* publicity brochure from East Kilbride Town Council and East Kilbride Development Corporation, 1967
[3] 'Aberdeen—spoiled child of Scotland' by Colin Maclean (TIMES EDUCATIONAL SUPPLEMENT, SCOTLAND 6 December 1974
[4] *Akenfield* by Ronald Blythe   (PENGUIN)

Causes
of Change

People are seldom employed out of charity. They are taken on to help with the production of some commodity or with the provision of a service. If the public's demand for that commodity or service falls, the number of job opportunities will inevitably fall. If some technical change (a change in the methods used for making the commodity or providing the service) reduces the need for labour to perform particular tasks, again there will be a decline in the numbers sought, at least in the short term.

In most industries, both changes in the *market* for goods and services and *technical* changes affect the number of jobs available. In some industries, on the other hand, one is markedly more in evidence than the other. Here market change implies changes beyond the control of the industry or firm; while technical change is initiated by the industry or firm.

Agriculture has enjoyed a post-war boom which bears comparison with the so-called agricultural revolution of the eighteenth and nineteenth centuries. Home production of most foodstuffs is much higher than it was twenty years ago. Overall output is nearly 60 per cent higher than in 1955. And yet the 1,100,000 people who made a living in farming in 1955 have dwindled to about 600,000 in 1975. In this, technical change is almost entirely the basic cause. Jobs that used to be done by men are now mechanized. Larger farms allow better use of manpower, and so the many amalgamations have led to redundancies.

In the provision of many services, especially those with a personal service element (where technological change can have only a limited impact), any fall in employment is almost entirely due to changes in market forces. Local passenger transport is a case in point. With the growth in private motoring, the 'taste' for public transport has declined, bringing with it an inevitable fall in the numbers recruited to man buses and suburban trains.

Contrasting cases: coal and cars

The spectacular decline of the coal industry is an example of an industry which has seen both influences at work simultaneously. The demand for coal has declined consistently from its peak in 1913. Since nationalization in 1947, huge investments in equipment and improved methods of coal-winning have reduced the labour requirements even further.

These two influences—the market and technology—often act together in a more favourable direction. A technical innovation can cut the cost of production of a commodity. If the price is cut as a result, this should induce an increase in the public's demand for that commodity. This was the case with the motor vehicle industry in the 1950s. The adoption of techniques of mass production brought about a relative cut in prices which helped to build up a mass demand for motor cars. Here, labour-saving developments brought about an expansion of output more than sufficient to maintain, and even expand the level of employment.

Again, a technical innovation may open up a new market, offering employment opportunities in jobs closely related to previous skills. This has happened with the cotton textile industry. The development of man-made fibres has allowed the British cotton industry to move into specialist fields to withstand the intense international competition in the mass market from low-cost producers of ordinary cotton piece-goods, such as India and Hong Kong.

MARKET CHANGES

Development of substitutes

The tremendous fall in coal production, charted in Table 2.1 is due to the development of a *substitute* for coal, in the form of oil and, to a lesser extent, as yet, nuclear energy and natural gas.

An earlier market blow to the fortunes of the coal industry came with the development of electricity. Although, as a secondary fuel, electricity was derived almost entirely from coal, it was a more efficient way of using the energy generated by burning coal than

	1913	1973
Production (*million tonnes*)	292	132
Labour force	1,127,000	257,000
Proportion of British energy requirements supplied by coal	100%	43%
Exports of coal (*million tonnes*)	100	3

Table 2.1   *Performance of the British coal industry, 1913 and 1973*

direct use of the coal. Thus, although the electricity supply industry is the National Coal Board's biggest customer by far, electricity is in a real sense one of coal's competitors in the market for energy.

The development of a substitute, or a technical development which enables that substitute to be produced more cheaply, is a recurrent theme in the pattern of British industrial change.

Sometimes the substitute is a development from existing products, and existing firms transfer resources from one product line to another—although this transition cannot be achieved overnight. This has been the case with the absorption of man-made fibres into the cotton textile industry.

At other times the substitute is fundamentally different, requiring different skills from work-people and needing completely different machinery. The change from steam boilers to electric motors in the first half of this century is an example of such a change, which brought about the almost total collapse of the older industry. The function of both products was the same, but they were different in every other way.

Loading for export—a rare sight.

Loss of overseas markets

Coal, like cotton, has fallen victim to one of the dangers inherent in Britain being a major trading nation—the loss, often suddenly, of export markets. Until the 1914–18 war, both coal and cotton were very important British exports. Trade was severely cut back during the hostilities for a number of reasons.

1 to release shipping for carrying vital war materials.

2 to allow cuts in production without harming supplies for Britain itself so that men and women could be released for the armed forces and munitions work.

3 because of the physical dangers of sinking by U-boats.

This meant that overseas customers had to find alternative sources of supply. In some cases they found U.S. or Japanese companies very willing to step in. In other cases, they developed a native industry.

In 1913, Lancashire cotton mills supplied 60 per cent of India's huge needs. During the war the small Indian cotton industry was developed. With 'protection' from competition afforded by the war, the Indian industry grew until it was able to compete more than favourably with the Lancashire mills. By 1937, over 80 per cent of Indian cotton requirements were home-produced, and they were even selling certain kinds of çotton in the British market.

The fillip to native industries which the war provided stood them in good stead for the intense competition for the greatly reduced world markets of the Depression years. Although coal and cotton stand out because of the spectacular nature of their collapse, many British industries' fortunes were very seriously damaged by the inter-war cutback in the volume of world trade. In many instances these industries were only in the 1970s adjusting to the problems set by that watershed in British economic history.

Competition in world markets

Demand from foreign buyers is always more 'volatile' than home demand. Competition abroad is usually fiercer. There is little consumer loyalty; purchasing will be on a strictly commercial basis. Importing business is usually in the hands of large-scale importers whose bulk purchases make even a small difference in price between firms in different countries attractive. Thus, if a firm lets its price rise even a little above that of a competitor producing an identical product it is likely to suffer a big drop in sales. However, where a firm is selling a product of which it is the sole supplier, sales abroad will be rather more stable since potential customers can turn to no one else. Such will be the case with highly specialized machinery or Scotch whisky.

Loss of savings from large-scale production

Any firm which sells a large part of its output abroad is subject to these risks. Further, producing large 'runs' can lead to significant savings in the cost of producing each product which would be lost if sales abroad fall.

Such a case is motor cars. A significant part of the cost of producing motor cars is the cost of tools and equipment used, e.g. *equipment and tool costs for a particular model work out at £200,000 per week. A production run of 2000 cars per week will mean that each car has to cover only £100 of these costs. A fall in overseas sales results in a cut in weekly production to 1250. But the cost of tools and equipment is unchanged at £200,000. Thus each car on the shortened production run must cover £160 of the equipment costs.*

This must affect the price that the motor vehicle firm charges for its cars. Such a price increase is bound to harm further their sales abroad and it may impair their competitiveness in the home market.

Changes in conditions in the home market

As the level of affluence of the country has increased, the patterns of consumer spending have changed greatly. The level of wages in 1975 was over sixteen times that of 1900. Although increases in the level of prices has somewhat reduced the benefits of that, the volume of consumers' spending is three times what it was at the beginning of the century.

Items	1953	1973
Food	30·5	18·9
Fuel and light	4·0	4·2
Durable goods (cars, furniture, electrical goods)	6·2	8·9
Running costs of vehicles	1·5	5·4
Holidays abroad	1·4	1·8

Table 2.2   *Percentage of consumer expenditure spent on various items, 1953 and 1973*

The proportion of this *extra* income which goes to food, and other necessities, has fallen; whilst other items have taken up a progressively larger share of this ever-larger income. The 'mass market' for consumer durable goods is largely a twentieth-century phenomenon. Many of the most dynamic industries in Britain are based entirely on personal consumption. Others are made commercially viable by the demand from industries producing items which are a result of greater general affluence, such as tyres. Important industries like motor vehicles, aircraft for passenger travel, electronic consumer goods like televisions, education, health and social services, tourism and catering are almost entirely creatures of twentieth-century affluence.

Greater spending power does not benefit all industries equally. The general public has turned away from using coal in the home because it is dirty and inconvenient. Since the 1950s they have turned towards oil, electricity or gas.

Another example of the perversity of consumer behaviour is the decline of fish, which has low status, at the hands of meat which has high status; or the demise of brown bread in favour of more fancied white bread—in contradiction to the nutritional value!

In general, therefore, the level of Britain's affluence has affected industries in different ways. On some, like motor vehicles, it has conferred the advantages of rapid growth. Others, like food processing, have had to content themselves with modest increases in consumer demand, while there are some cases, like coal, where demand has actually fallen.

TECHNICAL CHANGES

The Luddite riots of 1811–12 involved the smashing of new machinery in factories in the east Midlands of England. This was the angry reaction of domestic piece-workers at the undermining of their livelihood by the much more efficient power-looms of the emergent factories. New methods of working have always been met with suspicion.

Containers

The 'container revolution' is an example. A firm rents a large metal container, packs it and dispatches it to its destination, without the recurrent unloading and re-loading of the past. This is clearly more efficient in the use of manpower, and thus cheaper. Just as clearly, it means a reduction in the numbers needed to handle

It was never like this in Grandpa's day.

cargoes at ports and other transport depots. Many dockers are angry that, just at the time when they have won worthwhile breakthroughs in working conditions (with the de-casualization of labour in the industry), this clear threat to the livelihood of many of them has come upon them. Solutions will no doubt be worked out over time, such as using dockers to pack the containers at the beginning of their journey, but the suspicion that has grown up between dockers and employers over years of bitter conflict will make that process less than smooth.

Printing

The revolution in printing techniques is another case where great strides forward in printing technology, such as computer type-setting or web-offset printing, involve a cutback in the number of jobs involved. In an industry where the unions are strong and rewards are relatively high, there is a virtual guarantee of conflict. Clearly simple pleas of 'progress' will not impress work-people who are to be thrown out of well-paid employment.

In the longer term, of course, technical improvement does not invariably produce harmful effects.

1 *Boost in sales*

A new technique of production should allow more efficient production and thus lower unit costs. This should enable a boost in sales through lower prices. Higher sales will, in turn, push up the level of employment—perhaps to levels even higher than before the introduction of the technical change. This has been the case with motor vehicles and other consumer durable goods.

2 *Boost in related alternative employment*

Although a new method of working may reduce the numbers required in manufacturing, perhaps permanently, it may stimulate increased employment in servicing, such as transport, or in financial services, or in the production of components. The production of synthetic fibres has compensated to some degree for the loss of jobs in cotton spinning.

3 *Boost in public services*

In general, the release of men from one employment will allow the community to produce some of the other things that are wanted. The greater national income which should result from a technical improvement will allow the community's elected leaders to devote more to medical care, education, improving the environment and the quality of life generally.

The bulk of coal is now produced by machines like this Anderton Shearer.

Mechanization

The result of widespread mechanization, such as Britain has seen
in the years since the war, is that the *productivity* of labour (output
of the average workman) has gone up. This has produced the
'standard' pattern of lay-offs in the coal industry. Since 1947,
when it was nationalized, the coal industry has boosted labour
productivity by about two-and-a-half times, through the use
of power-loading, shearers, power tools and other mechanical
aids.

Why did the strong unions in the mines accept these lay-offs?
They did not accept without protest, and many miners feel that
they should never have accepted it. But the leadership of the
unions, especially the dominant National Union of Mineworkers
(N.U.M.), accepted that unless they could raise productivity,
prices would be so high that coal would lose out entirely to cheaper
oil. This could mean a much bigger and more rapid decline for
the industry than the planned reduction of the late 1950s and the
1960s. It is significant that when the market situation changed
in their favour after the substantial increases in world oil prices
after late 1973, the attitude of the reduced mining labour force
hardened.

The spectre of automation remains a long-term prospect for
most British industries. But U.S. experiences, and the U.S.A.'s

permanently high unemployment, are a warning of the severe effects of this more radical form of progress. While its benefits to us as consumers is potentially enormous, its impact on us as workers will be drastically to cut industrial employment.

Standardization

In 1946, 32 companies produced 367,000 motor vehicles in Britain. In 1973, just four companies produced 2,164,000 motor vehicles. This immense increase in sales was due partly to a reduction in prices resulting from the implementation of the techniques of mass production of standardized components.

This depends on the simple truth that the larger the number produced, the cheaper the cost of each—what economists call 'economies of large-scale production'. If you are undertaking large production runs of an identical product, it is worthwhile installing tools and machines to help to do the job, some parts of it automatically. These aids can produce more cheaply than men using only hand tools.

	1939	1960
Weekly output of cars	1700	6750
Workforce (approximate)	19,000	23,000
Average working week (hours)	52·5	42·5
Man-hours per car	587	145

Table 2.3   *The results of mass production at Austin Motors*

Table 2.3 shows the results of introducing standardized parts and mass production methods at Austin's Birmingham plant. It shows that the labour element in the production of a car was reduced by 75 per cent. This helped to bring the price down and boost sales. This, in turn boosted employment by over 20 per cent.

The same situation can be seen in other consumer durable goods industries. The production of standard parts in the 1950s enabled the price of refrigerators to be slashed. In 1973, an average refrigerator was 20 per cent *cheaper* than it had been in 1954. During this period, average earnings rose by four times. Not surprisingly, this had a favourable effect on the sales of fridges, and on employment in that industry. Sales in 1973 were 1,240,000 units compared to 430,000 in 1954—and over 70 per cent of British households had a refrigerator of their own in 1973.

Innovation

The twentieth century is full of examples of spectacular inventions which have been successfully exploited and have resulted in new industries, or at least new products. Some of the best known are the motor car, the aeroplane, artificial fibres, plastics, radio, TV, radar, the transistor, the hovercraft and the computer. Sometimes one has led to the other, as the discovery of the transistor in 1944 and the development of the micro-circuit in the early 1960s led to the commercial production of computers.

Sometimes an invention has replaced a less efficient commodity, as the car has replaced the horse-drawn carriage. At other times, an invention, such as computers, has allowed man to undertake tasks which were previously impossible. Other inventions have added to the range of industrial materials available, as plastics have done, without replacing existing materials. All have made new demands on labour, and offered new opportunities for jobs.

Research and development

About 1·8 per cent of Britain's national income, high by international standards, is devoted to research and development in industry. Firms—and Government, and industrial associations in some cases—spend a great deal of money (£710 million in 1969/70) trying to improve existing products, developing new versions of a basic model, looking for ways of making the same thing using fewer component parts and so on. The results of this expensive search for improvement and/or reductions in costs of production are less spectacular than the results of inventions. But they influence the sales of the product and thus the level of job opportunities. In some very competitive markets, as with artificial fibres, it is vital that new uses are found for products and that improvements are made, just to survive. The results of the research and development effort also have a material effect on the nature of jobs, requiring changes in skill, different work disciplines, the use of new tools or machines, shift working and so on.

In some cases, new developments create their own market. I.C.I. spent a great deal of money on their agricultural advisory service, for example, to persuade farmers of the usefulness of their chemical fertilizers in order to justify the large capital and research and development costs involved in getting production off the ground.

Work study

The techniques of work study are used to eliminate waste, cut down the number of processes involved, or locate machines and other equipment in the ideal place for speedy production. These also affect a firm's costs and so its competitive position.

Organization

In 1968, three firms—General Electric Company (G.E.C.), Associated Electrical Industries (A.E.I.) and the English Electric Company—merged, with Government encouragement. They had previously competed in many electrical engineering markets. It was felt that considerable economies could be won by better co-ordination of the production of these three large firms, making the British electrical engineering industry stand up more effectively to competition. By concentrating production of certain products on certain factories, it was possible to cut costs.

The three constituent firms had 265,000 employees when they merged. By the time the 'rationalization' was completed in 1971, this work force had been reduced by 36,000 and a further 40,000 were in different jobs or even in different factories. Of the 151 factories or plants involved in the merger, 39 were closed down.

During the 1960s many pits where the production costs were high were closed down and production concentrated on those pits where a significant degree of mechanization, and thus lower costs, was possible. This put many men out of work in some areas.

In their 1972 modernization plan, the British Steel Corporation announced their intention to close many of the small steel-making plants under their control and concentrate production in larger mills. Very considerable savings are possible by making steel in large, integrated steel mills (where all processes are on the same site). These mills do not need as many men to produce a tonne of steel as the smaller ones do. The result is that jobs are to be lost, even though B.S.C. plans to increase total output.

In the case of both coal and steel, the search for methods of keeping down costs was brought about by competition. In the case of coal, oil was the rival. In the case of steel, steel produced in the immense, low-cost European Community mills is the rival. If the British steel industry does not keep costs down, its prices will be undercut and employment will suffer.

Consequences of Change

Industrial change is seen by many as a treadmill in that it is impossible to quit once you have joined it. Unless British firms try to cut costs to keep their prices competitive, British markets may be flooded by cheaper foreign produce.

The only way to try to avoid this is for Britain to cut itself off behind prohibitive tariff walls. This is almost inconceivable. Britain imports so much of its basic foodstuffs and raw materials for industry, and currency must be earned from export sales to cover at least these. It is quite at odds with the trends of recent history.

By producing in a large market, where large sales are possible, significant economies can be earned by producing on a large scale, as seen in the cases of motor vehicles and steel in the previous chapter. This is the basic rationale behind the trading groups of which Britain has been a member—the European Free Trade Area (EFTA) and the more ambitious European Communities [European Economic Community (Common Market); European Coal and Steel Community (E.C.S.C.); European Atomic Energy Authority (Euratom)]. It is also behind moves to reduce barriers to international trade through negotiations within the General Agreement on Tariffs and Trade (GATT).

Economic progress has been characterized by ever-greater specialization. If Britain were to spread its resources to try to provide for all needs—which would have to happen if Britain withdrew from the international economy—it would lead to considerable inefficiency.

Many problems do emerge from the ever-changing pattern of industrial activity. But it is clear that trying to stop this change by cutting British industry off is counter-productive.

It is also true that benefits come from industrial change. More efficient methods of production allow more to be produced by the existing work force. This, not the money incomes that we pay to ourselves, increases the level of affluence that the country can enjoy. We can either consume what we produce or use some of it to buy the products of other countries.

Economic growth is also a way of side-stepping the awkward issues which result from the uneven distribution of wealth. You need not take from the 'haves' to give to the 'have-nots', you produce more so that you can increase the share for the formerly deprived without depriving the formerly privileged. However appealing this may be, especially to politicians anxious to offend no one, it is no panacea—the gap between the relative shares of 'rich' and 'poor' remains stubbornly wide.

It can be seen also in a world context, as rich countries try to justify the imbalance between rich and poor by putting all efforts into increasing 'global product'. That the distribution of this 'extra' product is just as hideously uneven as before reflects the reality that even the rich have so many pressing material demands that they feel able to perpetuate the situation.

More positively, economic growth enables more material wants to be satisfied, whether these are private, like alleviation of poverty, or public, like better health care, schools or housing.

The drawbacks of changes in industry, like the decline of the Durham pit villages, or the dislocation of life styles brought about by the oil industry, are more in evidence than the advantages. It does appear that we rapidly become accustomed to the benefits of material progress while its resulting hardships or inconveniences linger in our consciousness.

Whatever the problems implicit in the 'onward march of progress', it seems to be an inevitable aspect of the age. Indeed the pace of change in industry is increasingly rapid.

Since it is impossible to *avoid* industrial change, it is well to be aware of its consequences, so that action may be taken to remedy, and perhaps even avoid its worst aspects.

NEW SKILLS REQUIRED

As old industries decline, new industries are expanding. At times of economic depression, as during the inter-war period of the

1920s and 1930s, these two movements are not simultaneous. There is no mystical guarantee that the men made redundant by the decline of some industries on Friday will be absorbed by the expansion of new industries on Monday. The history of capitalist enterprise is one of fluctuations in the level of economic activity, usually labelled 'booms' and 'slumps'. A great deal of Government effort in the post-war era has concerned ways by which the economy may be 'managed' so as to maintain full employment.

Even if the chronological gap between the decline of the old and the expansion of the new can be avoided, the problem remains that the new industries will require different skills.

Re-training

The skills and the work disciplines which stood a man in good stead in the manufacture of steam boilers will be inappropriate to the manufacture of electric motors. Clearly people have to learn new skills and accustom themselves to new working conditions.

In 1974, 49,000 people went through one of the six-month courses offered in one of the 54 *Skillcentres* or Government Training Centres run by the Training Services Agency of the Manpower Services Commission. In six months, these people tried to absorb the essence of trades which normally require an apprenticeship of four or five years. Over 50 different trades are catered for.

Very few skilled men, however, go through systematic re-training. Once the status of 'skilled man' has been earned (through apprenticeship), it is transferred to other jobs in other trades. This must restrict the choice of alternative jobs to those where there is a fair measure of overlap with existing skills.

That few men who already have a skill for which they have 'served their time' volunteer for the Government re-training courses reveals that pride is involved when it comes to changing jobs. It is not enough to offer adequate financial inducements to undergo the six-month courses. Some of the *Skillcentres* now offer 'sponsored training' to men who are sent by a firm to update or add to their skills. This appears to be more acceptable to men who have skills already.

If Britain is to equip its work-people with the flexibility that rapid industrial change entails, it is necessary to learn from these experiences.

Industrial training

The death of old industries and the rise of new ones is not the only aspect of industrial change that affects the nature of work. Constant innovation, as a result of research and development and work study, and new machinery and tools mean that the nature of a job, even in the same industry, is always changing. The 'tricks of the trade' that used to be picked up during an apprenticeship will no longer last a skilled man, even though he may stay in the same industry, throughout his working life.

The object of training nowadays is to instil an understanding of the theory or principles involved in the tasks for which training is given. In this way constantly changing tasks or new tools can be mastered more easily.

In many industries it is common for apprentices to spend one day a week, or several weeks in a year, at a technical or further education college. These day-release or block-release courses usually lead to awards from the City and Guilds of London Institute. They complement the practical training given by the firm itself. But less than 25 per cent of each age group gets the opportunity to attend these courses, and the proportion is significantly lower for girls. In some industries any and all training that is given is within the firm where, normally, only the practical and short-term instruction is given.

To improve co-ordination in the field of industrial training, the Industrial Training Act 1964 allows for the establishment of Industrial Training Boards for groups of industries, financed by a levy on all firms in that industry. The 27 boards that have been set up—covering 85 per cent of those work-people in the industries to which the Act refers—make grants to those firms which offer courses of training approved by the board.

Mobility of labour between jobs

Notwithstanding more flexible initial training and the work of the *Skillcentres*, there are still many barriers standing in the way of easy transfer from one job to another.

The abilities required for certain jobs are not evenly spread throughout the population. These vary from height requirements for a policeman, through the well-developed sense of balance that a ballet dancer needs, to the mental capacities of a university professor or the personality characteristics needed to be a teacher of the deaf.

Although the *Skillcentres* now offer training in more than 50 trades, there are still many jobs where a long training is required and where it is impossible or very hard to come to it in later life. The seven years training of a medical practitioner may, by its very length, deter many.

The status of a job may be a deterrent factor. People will often be reluctant to change to a job which they regard as socially inferior to the one they have, or have had. Thus a skilled man may be less than eager to accept a job as a machine minder. The opposite also holds true in some cases. The 'right background' is still expected of candidates for some jobs. Very few doctors or lawyers are recruited from the ranks of the working class in Britain. The further a job is from one's experience, the less will be known about it and how to go about getting any qualifications that may be needed.

In spite of the Sex Discrimination Act 1975 and the Equal Opportunities Commission set up under its provisions, some jobs are still regarded in the popular imagination as 'women's' and others as 'men's'. A few jobs are closed to one sex (like underground work in pits to women) by law.

CHANGED WORKING CONDITIONS

Every day, in the United States, 65 car workers drop dead at their jobs on the factory floor: on average, some 16,000 of them die in the plants every year, and over half of these have heart attacks. Add to these figures—which do NOT include the results of accidents at work—the 63,000 cases of disabling diseases, and the 1,700,000 cases of lost or impaired hearing, and you realize that the car industry wreaks as heavy a toll on the American working class as did the Vietnam war.[1]

The motor car industry is the classic case of 'de-skilling' whereby jobs are reduced to their barest essentials to allow mechanization of the standard processes, leaving the 'human element' in the assembly line with a simple, crushingly boring task.

Work in the motor industry is occasionally dangerous; often it is hot, or dusty, or smelly, or noisy; but always it is tedious, demanding a watchful dexterity and a nervous endurance to carry out monotonous, fatiguing operations time after time

An assembly conveyor at Chrysler's Linwood plant near Glasgow.

after time. Few of the jobs demand any skill of the people doing them. As early as 1925 Henry Ford estimated that 79 per cent of all new recruits could be made proficient in eight days and that 45 per cent needed only a day's 'training'.[1]

The effects of this type of work are without any advantage. Sometimes, they are spectacular.

James Johnson worked for Chrysler at its axle plant at Elsdon in the United States. After a dispute with the foreman, he left the plant returning with a shotgun which he used to kill two foremen and a job setter. The defence lawyer claimed that the working conditions at Elsdon were such that Johnson could not be held responsible for his actions. The judge and jury visited the plant, found the situation there 'abominable', and agreed that Johnson was temporarily insane at the time of the killings.[1]

The catalogue of the inhumanities of work on the assembly lines of the motor vehicle and other industries is already vast and growing. An official of the Work Research Unit of the Department of Employment has said that:

low motivation exists in a lot of firms in British industry, because people are not involved in their work. This leads to a lot of real problems such as low productivity, absenteeism, high labour turnover and industrial unrest. We are predicting that these things will get worse if changes are not thought about now.[1]

In Sweden, the two motor manufacturers—Saab and Volvo—have long had problems recruiting and especially keeping workers, despite high wages. The firms have been forced to introduce a scheme whereby a gang of workmen tackle a range of assembly jobs at their own speed. In Italy, Fiat employees are demanding the right to negotiate the speed of the 'track'.

The subordination of man to the machine is all too common a theme in the annals of twentieth-century industrial 'progress'. This alienation is hardly helped by the growing concentration of British industry into larger and larger units. The man who works on the shop floor is more distant than ever before from those who make boardroom decisions—and this appears to be the same in publicly-owned concerns (nationalized industries) as in large private firms. The day of the family firm, where the owner took an interest, however patronizingly, in individual employees, has passed out of the folklore and, largely, from reality.

The mindlessness of modern work has given a fillip to demands for worker control, or at least a greater say in the choice of production techniques.

REGIONAL IMBALANCE IN JOB OPPORTUNITIES

Table 3.1 shows that some parts of Britain have consistently suffered from worse unemployment than others. Northern Ireland, Scotland, Wales, the north and the north-west of England and, to a lesser extent, Yorkshire and Humberside have had rates of unemployment higher than the national average. With rare exceptions, the five regions in the south and east of Britain have enjoyed lower rates of unemployment than the U.K. average.

There is nothing new about this. At the height of the economic depression of the 1930s, when the national rate of unemployment was at the staggering figure of 22·1 per cent, some regions were markedly worse off than others. Wales had a rate of 36·5 per cent—more than one in three was out of work. Some 28 per cent of the Scottish work force was without work. The rate was 28·5 per

Region	1960	1965	1970	1975
Scotland	3·6	3·0	4·3	5·3
Wales	2·7	2·6	4·0	5·8
Northern Ireland	6·7	6·1	7·0	8·0
England:				
North	2·9	2·6	4·8	6·0
North-west	1·9	1·6	2·8	5·4
Yorkshire and Humberside	(1·1*)	1·1	2·9	4·1
East Midlands		0·9	2·3	3·8
West Midlands	1·0	0·9	2·3	4·4
South-west	1·7	1·6	2·8	5·0
East Anglia	(1·0*)	1·3	2·1	3·7
South-east		0·9	1·7	3·0
United Kingdom	1·7	1·5	2·7	4·3

* In 1960, figures for Yorkshire and Humberside and East Midlands; and for East Anglia and South-east are combined.

Table 3.1   *Rate of unemployment in the regions of the U.K., 1960–75, shown as percentages of work force*

cent in the north-east of England, and 26 per cent in the north-west. And yet, in London and the south-east it was 'only' 13·5 per cent. Within these large regions, there were pockets where the rate went even higher. When Palmer's ship repair yard closed its gates in the Tyneside town of Jarrow in 1933, no fewer than eight out of every ten workers in the town were out of a job.

In 1960, the Scottish Council (Development and Industry) appointed a committee under Sir John Toothill to look into the state of the Scottish economy to try to explain the consistently higher level of unemployment there than for the U.K. as a whole. The committee found that the early years of rapid economic growth in Scotland, in the nineteenth century, was a time of heavy specialization on industries which are now in decline.

> Scotland has substantially more of the declining industries, and is weak in the newer growing industries such as science-based industries and a wide range of consumers' and consumer durable manufacturing industries.[2]

Thus, as the industries whose labour needs are falling laid men off, there were not enough new firms to hire the unemployed.

The six industries listed in Table 3.2 as 'declining' have been cutting down on their work forces. They are all over-represented in Scotland. Between them they accounted for 31·9 per cent of all

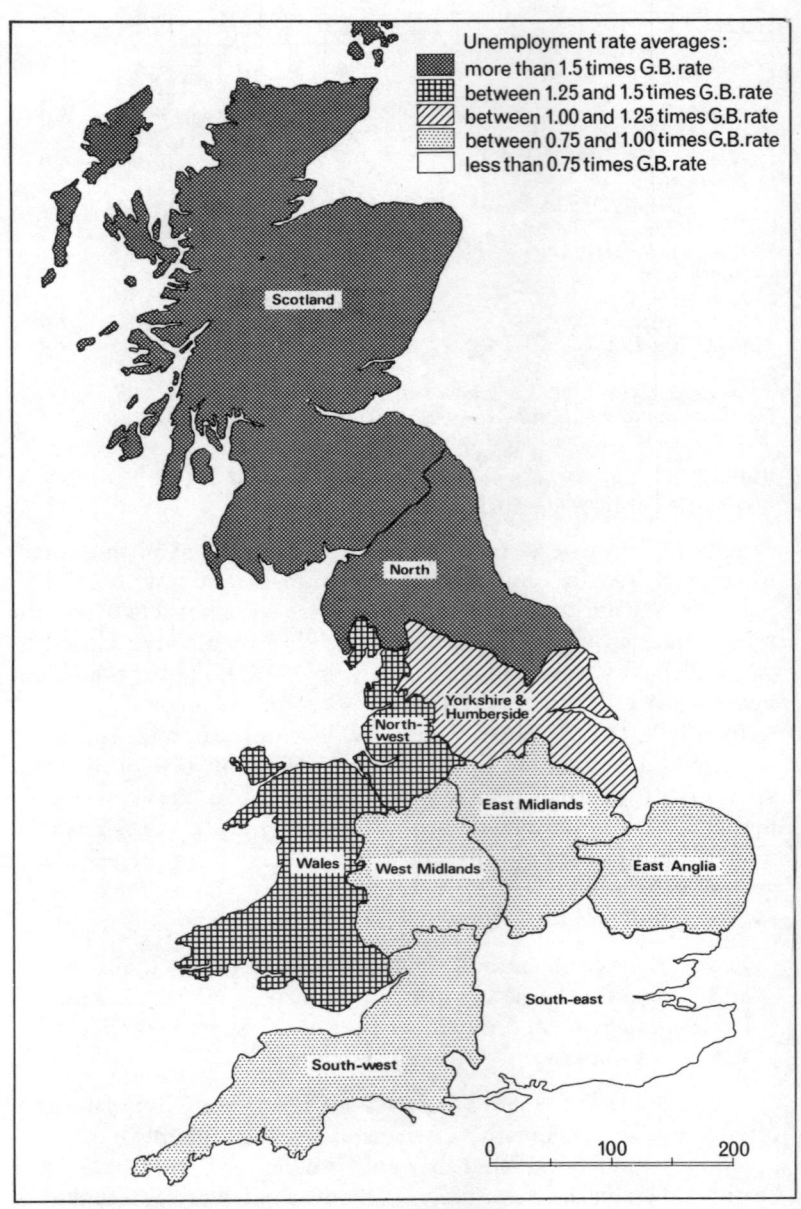

Unemployment rate averages:
- more than 1.5 times G.B. rate
- between 1.25 and 1.5 times G.B. rate
- between 1.00 and 1.25 times G.B. rate
- between 0.75 and 1.00 times G.B. rate
- less than 0.75 times G.B. rate

Scotland

North

Yorkshire & Humberside

North-west

East Midlands

Wales

West Midlands

East Anglia

South-east

South-west

0   100   200

Regional differences in the rate of unemployment.

Industries	Scottish work force	U.K. work force
Declining		
Agriculture	3·2	1·8
Coal mining	2·3	2·2
Shipbuilding and marine engineering	2·2	0·9
Textiles	4·3	3·2
Transport and communications	7·2	6·9
Distributive trades	12·7	12·2
Expanding		
Engineering and electrical goods	8·7	9·9
Financial, business, professional and scientific services	15·0	14·6
Miscellaneous services	8·2	9·3
Motor vehicles	1·8	3·5

Table 3.2 *Scotland's share of declining and expanding industries, 1968, shown as percentage of work force*

Scottish jobs in 1968, compared to only 27·2 per cent of employment for the U.K. as a whole.

The four industries described as 'expanding' have been adding to their work forces in Scotland. All but professional and scientific services are under-represented in Scotland. Between them they accounted for 33·7 per cent of Scottish jobs in 1968, compared to 37·3 per cent of employment for the whole U.K.

With variations, much the same situation can be found in the other five relatively depressed regions of the northern and western parts of Britain.

EMIGRATION AND DE-POPULATION

The inevitable result of the failure of the newer, expanding industries to build their factories in sufficient numbers in those regions where declining industries have been shedding labour is that people have left the relatively depressed regions. In 1965/66, 40,000 more people left Scotland than went to settle there, and the population actually fell.

In 1921 the regions of the north and west held 49·9 per cent of Britain's population. Although none has actually lost population, they have failed to provide for the whole of their natural increase (of births over deaths) over the years. Their share of Britain's population in 1971 was down to 43·7 per cent.

Region	1921	1971
Scotland	11·1	9·4
Wales	6·0	4·9
Northern Ireland	2·9	2·8
England:		
North	6·9	5·9
North-west	13·7	12·1
Yorkshire and Humberside	9·3	8·6
East Midlands	5·3	6·1
West Midlands	8·0	9·2
South-west	6·2	6·8
East Anglia	2·8	3·0
South-east	28·0	31·0
	100·0	100·0

Table 3.3   *Percentage of U.K. population in major regions, 1921 and 1971*

Causes of emigration

Consistently higher unemployment has made the prospects bleak in the depressed regions. With less work and thus less overtime, earnings are rather lower in the depressed regions than they are in the south. Although the gap is small in practice, people *think* that it is wide. The legacy of old industry—coal tips, industrial waste, grime, the bitter attitudes resulting from long struggle—makes life in parts of the depressed areas less attractive to some than the 'softer', relatively unspoiled south. The lure of London is an age-old factor which plays its part still.

The complex of feelings, truths and half-truths that eventually drive someone to pull up their roots and move to a new area or even go abroad are hard to explain. But many people have moved. The exodus has not approached the tremendous movement of humanity within Italy, from the unimaginably poor south to the affluent north. But it has made a difference both to the area they left, and to the area to which they go in search of a new life.

Effects of emigration

The young tend to be more mobile than the elderly or even those in their thirties, who have family commitments, who may have a house after long years on a waiting list, whose kids are in school and among friends they would be reluctant to leave, as would their parents. Emigration tends to leave behind an ageing population. Those with skills to offer are also more mobile than those who lack them. Emigration tends to leave a disproportionately unskilled population behind.

Emigration sets off a vicious circle. For every family which leaves, a job in the service industries—in shops, entertainment, educational or medical services—is lost. If that person leaves, yet another job is lost and so on.

Social life is bound to suffer with the loss of those who are young and whose skills mean that they are better paid than average. Facilities in the community often suffer as earning power is reduced; the retired and lower-paid unskilled people who remain are not able to keep up clubs, parks, streets and so on. It is a paradox, which is not lost on those tempted to move away, that the most depressed areas generally bear the heaviest rates burdens.

An air of dilapidation, of depression, feeds upon itself. The lack of facilities drives out the young people as soon as they are able to go. There is nothing to attract any businessman to set up a factory in the community, and so the process of decay goes on unchecked.

This is very much the pattern of the dying pit villages of Durham, and of so many other places. For all their beauty, the description would fit the Highlands of Scotland, the Lake District or the rugged mountains of mid-Wales.

Local emigration

This process of emigration is not only a movement over large areas. There is continual movement over short distances, and from countryside to town, and vice versa. Nor does movement affect all areas equally.

Region	1921	1971
Highlands and Islands (p)	5·3	4·4
Grampian (p)	9·0	8·4
Tayside (p)	8·0	7·6
Fife	6·0	6·3
Central	4·3	5·2
Lothians	13·0	14·5
Strathclyde	49·2	49·0
Dumfries and Galloway (p)	2·9	2·7
Borders (p)	2·3	1·8
	100·0	100·0

Table 3.4 *Percentage of Scottish population in the regions of Scotland, 1921 and 1971*

Table 3.4 shows the marked redistribution which has taken place *within* Scotland in the last generation. In 1921 the five 'peripheral' regions in the north and in the south—indicated by (*p*) in the table—held 27·5 per cent of Scotland's people. By 1971, their share had fallen to 24·9 per cent. The Highlands and Islands, Grampian, the Borders and Dumfries and Galloway actually had a lower population in 1971 than in 1921.

Changes in the location of industry have thus had a very marked effect on the distribution of Britain's population, with serious social consequences for the areas which have lost people, and, in some ways, no less serious problems of congestion for many of the areas which have taken them in.

---

[1] 'Car Making: an industry at war with its workers' by Huw Benyon (NEW SOCIETY 12 June 1975)

[2] Toothill Report 1961, paragraph 23:16 H.M.S.O.

Diversification

Nineteenth-century industrial growth

The period of rapid economic change, which we call the Industrial Revolution, was based on the production of 'intermediate' and 'capital' goods. Cotton was 'king'; coal, iron and later steel, the engineering group of industries (especially shipbuilding, railway stock, textile machinery, machine tools, steam engines) were the backbone of the growing modern sector of the economy throughout the nineteenth century. Only brewing, pottery, some of the Birmingham metal trades and a few other newly mechanized industries served the domestic consumer directly.

The giant capital goods industries clustered on the coalfields of Britain. They gravitated there because of the need for coal as fuel for the engines to make steam which drove the machinery in the new factories. Thus the coal-bearing areas—central Scotland, the north-east of England, Yorkshire–Notts–Derbyshire, Lancashire, the Black Country of south Staffordshire, north Staffordshire and south Wales—became the forcing ground for these industries.

Industrial collapse between the wars

The export-oriented, nineteenth-century economy crashed in ruins in the world depression after 1918.

Between 1912 and 1938 the quantity of cotton cloth made in Britain fell from 8000 million to barely 3000 million square yards; the amount exported from 7000 million to less than 1500 million square yards. Never since 1851 had Lancashire exported so little. Between 1854 and 1913 the output of British

35

coal had grown from 65 to 287 million tons. By 1938 it was down to 227 million and still falling. In 1913 twelve million tons of British shipping had sailed the seas, in 1938 there was rather less than eleven million. British shipyards in 1870 built 343,000 tons of vessels for British owners, and in 1913 almost a million tons: in 1938 they built little more than half a million.[1]

The human devastation of mass unemployment, resulting from this industrial collapse

stamped the years between the wars indelibly with the mark of bitterness and poverty. . . .

In 1913–14, about three per cent of the workers in Wales had been unemployed—rather less than the national average. In 1934—after recovery had begun—37 per cent of the labour force in Glamorgan, 36 per cent of that in Monmouth, were out of work. Two-thirds of the men of Ferndale, three-quarters of those in Brynmawr, Dowlais and Blaina, 70 per cent of those in Merthyr, had nothing to do except stand at street corners and curse the system that put them there.[1]

	1913	1938
Cotton cloth production (millions of square metres)	6690*	2510
Cotton cloth exports (millions of square metres)	2510*	1250
Employment in cotton	621,000*	288,000
Coal production (millions of tonnes)	292	231
Tonnes of British shipping at sea	12m	less than 11m
Tonnage of shipping launched from British yards	nearly 1,000,000	just over 500,000

1912

Table 4.1 *The Statistics of Gloom*

Over-reliance on a single staple industry

The tragedy of putting 'all your eggs in one basket' could be clearly seen.

The grimy, roaring, black industrial areas of the nineteenth century—in northern England, Scotland and Wales—had never been very beautiful or comfortable, but they had been active and prosperous. Now all that remained was the grime, the bleakness and the terrible silence of the factories and mines which did not work, the shipyards which were closed.[1]

The cry was to *diversify*, to provide a variety or diversity of employment opportunities in an area. If one industry did collapse, it would not have the tragic effects that befell those many areas of the industrial heartland of the nineteenth century which specialized in one, or a closely related group of industries, ruined after 1918.

This fact is easier to discover than to remedy. The Toothill Report observed that:

a given industry may be expected to adapt itself to change provided the change is not too drastic in terms of the industry's technology and trading practices.... There have been managements which have successfully made the change but these are exceptional, in Scotland and elsewhere. ... New industries in Britain and probably in other countries have tended to come largely from new men and not from the older established manufacturing concerns.[2]

New succeeds old—but in the wrong place

Many new industries based on sales to the consumer grew up during the 1920s and 1930s. For those in work, the period between the wars was one of increasing prosperity, if always against a background of fear of sudden and prolonged unemployment, and though very unevenly distributed. Technical improvements, especially the introduction of mass production methods, had brought the price of many goods within the reach of many ordinary working people.

The discovery of the mass market was not new. What was new was the visible contrast between the flourishing home market industries and the despairing exporters, symbolized in the contrast between an expanding Midlands and south-east, and a depressed north and west. In a broad belt stretching between the Birmingham and London regions, industry grew: the new motor manufacture was virtually confined to this zone. The new consumer-goods factories multiplied along the Great West Road out of London, while emigrants from Wales and the north moved to Coventry and Slough. Industrially, Britain was turning into two nations.[1]

Post-war unemployment, even in the relatively depressed regions, bears no comparison with pre-war levels. Although there has been no solution to the imbalance exemplified in Table 3.2, there have been successes.

ADJUSTMENTS BY EXISTING INDUSTRIES

Diversity does not mean only variety of industries. It certainly does not mean that traditional industries have no place in the economy of an area. To encourage the diversity of *products* offered by an industry is another aim. If one 'line' falls into disfavour with the consumers, others may hold up, or new lines may be brought to the market. The effects of falling demand for one of a number of products are clearly less harmful than the loss of sales of a sole product.

Sheffield is one of the oldest steel-making centres in Britain. In the form of billets, bars, rods, wire, sheet and strip steel, the steel mills of Sheffield–Rotherham–Stocksbridge provide a large proportion of the steel used by manufacturing industry in Britain, especially the motor vehicle industry. But they are also responsible for almost all the British production of stainless steel and a very high proportion of other alloy steels also. The British Steel Corporation and the remaining private firms are both heavily involved in the production of 'heavy forgings and castings' for industrial plant, such as power stations. The very hard steels needed for tools, both hand tools and machine tools, are produced almost exclusively by Sheffield's private steel firms. The long-famous cutlery trade continues there. The many small private firms in the area 'finish' steel which has been made elsewhere for a hundred and one specialist uses. Thus the steel industry of South Yorkshire operates in many different markets. It is highly improbable that all will collapse at the same time.

Many traditional industries whose work forces are now far smaller than they were twenty years ago can still be judged successful. The market for their 'staple' has been disappearing, or they have been unable to compete with low-cost producers elsewhere. And yet they have not disappeared. They have found a new place for themselves, perhaps in a 'slimmer' version. But they have retained jobs in an area which they would have failed to do without diversifying into new products.

Cotton

After the war, it was hard to find anyone seriously to doubt the prediction that the Lancashire cotton industry, once at the forefront of the world's first industrial revolution, would soon be extinct.

This is something that Lancashire viewed in two ways. The old brigade tended to 'hope it would never happen', while the more realistic managements expected it to happen, planned for it, and switched to synthetics just as quickly as possible. So the textile industry has shrunk and the number of units in it has been drastically reduced with a small number of giants and a larger number of specialist and independent units.[3]

The expertise that used to produce cotton piece-goods has been turned towards the production of artificial fibres and their incorporation, with cotton, into composite fabrics. The industry now specializes in high-quality cotton–polyester products. It is highly mechanized, using technology which is rapidly changing. The vast finance needed, and the much greater co-ordination required between the various stages in the production of cotton cloth, have resulted in a spate of mergers. The industry is now dominated by large groups, such as Courtaulds, Carrington Vyella, Tootal, Vantona. They are in a much stronger position to face competition from abroad than in the late 1950s.

Textile machinery

In 1945, Blackburn alone exported more looms than the whole of the well-developed Swiss textile machinery industry. But as the cotton industry in Lancashire declined, this industry's worldwide importance fell away. It survives, however, on a smaller scale. It makes machinery for producing 'texturized filament yarn' (nylon or polyester 'thread') and for other new processes. Platt International Ltd of Accrington has developed a radical new system of 'open end' spinning which is much more efficient than the traditional 'ring' spinning. The industry is far from dead or hanging on to past glories in an effort to stave off death. It is constantly on the look out for new markets for new products.

Wool

Although the woollen textiles industry of West Yorkshire was not affected so spectacularly as the cotton industry to the west of the Pennines, it has suffered from similar difficulties to a lesser degree. It has adopted similar solutions to those of Lancashire. The incorporation of artificial fibres has been so great that there is more man-made than natural fibre in most woollen goods. The industry concentrates on a range of specialized products which the highly mechanized firms in the industry can sell against overseas competition. The firms involved—like Coats Paton—have become larger, and control all stages in the production process. The work force, though reduced from previous levels when the industry competed in the bulk woollen piece-goods market, is now stable.

GROWTH OF MINOR INDUSTRIES

About 41 per cent of all employees in Great Britain work in the five relatively depressed regions of the British mainland—Scotland, Wales, northern England, the north-west of England, Yorkshire and Humberside.

Yet only 23·8 per cent of all jobs in the rapidly expanding, science-based instrument engineering industry are in these five regions. Conversely, 65·6 per cent of all jobs in the rapidly declining shipbuilding industry are located in the northern or western parts of Great Britain.

This is symptomatic of the regional imbalance in job opportunities that exists in Britain. But it should not obscure the very real progress that has been made in attracting new and expanding industries to the relatively depressed regions.

Chemicals in the north-west

No less than 72·4 per cent of jobs in general chemicals production, and 83·3 per cent in dye-stuffs manufacture are in the depressed regions. Indeed the north-west and the north-east of England are easily the most important of the many areas of Britain for the chemicals industry in general.

To some extent it is false to describe the chemicals industry as 'new' to the north-west or to the north-east. In many ways, its importance in these areas can be traced to the fact that they were important areas in the days when virtually the sole chemicals industry was the preparation of alkalis for soap and glass making. Merseyside rapidly became the most important centre for this industry because of the salt deposits of Cheshire and the limestone from the Peak District of north Derbyshire.

Another of the early uses for.chemicals was in the metal trades. The production of sulphuric acid, used in these trades, tended to go hand in hand with the production of soda. Many chemical products required other chemicals to bring them into being. There was thus a very high degree of interdependence of the various branches of the infant industry. Those areas which had an early importance tended to retain that advantage as more and more chemical compounds were added to the industry's repertoire. The expansion into petro-chemicals—chemicals derived from the refining of crude oil—after 1942 was a very expensive venture. It was possible only for those firms which were already well-established, who could thereby combine expertise and the ability to raise the huge sums needed to exploit it.

Almost every conceivable chemical product can be found in the many plants in the Manchester and Liverpool regions. More than a quarter of the chemicals industry's employees—117,000 in fact—work in the north-west. They produce well over half of all British-produced soap and detergents, a third of general chemicals (both organic and inorganic) and a quarter of all dye-stuffs. I.C.I. dominates here, as it does throughout the industry. Other prominent firms are CIBA-Geigy, B.P. Chemicals, Shell Chemicals, Albright & Wilson, Fisons, Unilever Chemicals, Burmah–Castrol, Glaxo, Laporte Industries and Kodak.

EMERGENCE OF NEW INDUSTRIES

Aircraft

The aircraft industry is a new industry. It is also one where the five northern and western regions of Britain are under-represented. They have only 29·7 per cent of the jobs in the industry. The largest number of these jobs is at the huge British Aircraft Corporation plants in Preston, which are mainly engaged in the production of military aircraft. The Hawker-Siddeley plant at Brough on Humberside is likewise engaged largely in military work. Rolls-Royce, the publicly-owned, sole aero-engine firm in Britain, has two plants near Glasgow and one at Barnoldswick in Yorkshire. There are, in addition, several small plants providing component parts or engaged in highly specialized market sectors throughout the depressed regions.

Motor vehicles

There is likewise under-representation for the relatively depressed regions in the motor vehicle industry, where they have only 27·5 per cent of the industry's jobs. But the north-west is *the* major centre for production of buses and lorries. The British Leyland plants at Leyland and Chorley in Lancashire and the bus plant at Workington in Cumbria employ 9500. Fodens and E.R.F., the two main independent truck producers, operate in Cheshire. Trucks are also produced by British Leyland in Glasgow (Albion Motors) and near Bathgate. The industry has been very reluctant, however, to establish its motor car assembly plants out-

Assembly line for commercial vehicles at Leyland in Lancashire.

side the West Midlands and the south-east. After considerable Government pressure in the 1960s, Ford established a plant at Halewood near Liverpool, and Vauxhall built another across the Mersey at Ellesmere Port, which employ 30,000 people between them; and they have attracted several firms of component suppliers also. The Chrysler plant at Linwood, built by Rootes in 1963 before their absorption by the U.S. firm, employed nearly 8000 people until the major re-organization of Chrysler in 1976.

Electronics in Scotland

The electronics industry is one of the most rapidly expanding in Britain. Scotland has established itself as the second most important area, after London and the south-east. Many of the big national, and international firms have plants scattered throughout Scotland—for the production of capital equipment from computers to navigational aids, including measuring and testing equipment, and defence equipment; for the production of electronic components, both active, like valves, semi-conductors and integrated

Some products new to the 1970s have made a significant contribution to widening job opportunities.

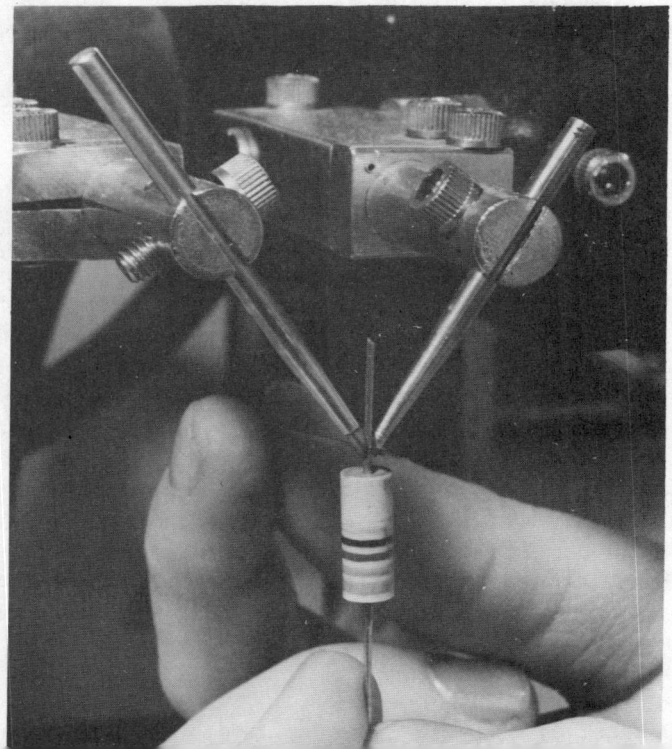

circuits, and passive, like gramophone turntables. Some of the larger producers are Plessey at Bathgate, S.T.C. (Standard Telephones and Cables) at East Kilbride, Hewlett-Packard at South Queensferry, Edinburgh, Beckman Instruments at Glenrothes, General Instruments, also at Glenrothes and G.E.C. at Glenrothes and Kirkcaldy.

Electronic business systems are well-represented, by Burroughs at Cumbernauld, N.C.R. (National Cash Register) in Dundee and Honeywell Controls at Newhouse near Glasgow.

There are many small, local firms producing particular components or highly specialized electronic systems, like M.E.S.L. (Microwave and Electronic Systems Ltd) of Newbridge, Midlothian, who have developed an electronic security system.

The largest concern of all is Ferranti. It has 5400 employees in six plants in the east of Scotland. Its three Edinburgh plants concentrate on defence work, in the field of 'avionics' (electronics for the aviation industry), including a major contribution to the joint British–German–Italian multi-rôle combat aircraft (M.R.C.A.). The Dalkeith plant produces measurement and inspection equipment for use with advanced machine tools. The Dundee plant is involved in the production of a wide range of components, and in the developments in 'laser' beam control equipment.

SWING TO SERVICE INDUSTRIES

In any account, even one as selective as this, of success in diversifying industry in the traditional industrial areas of Britain, some mention must be made of the large number of new jobs which have been created in the relatively depressed regions of Britain in the service industries. There has been a relative swing nationally from manufacturing towards service industries, and the relatively depressed regions have shared in this. Many new jobs have been created in the educational and medical services. Catering has grown very rapidly as the level of general affluence has grown. Tourism has been established as a vital industry in some parts of the country, such as the Scottish Highlands, where there is little alternative employment.

The 1973 Hardman Report, which recommended the dispersal of 31,000 civil service jobs from London, has shown another

The great expansion of services, both business and personal, have made a major impact on the diversification of employment opportunities. This view of Manchester city centre shows the central library (round building) and the many new office blocks which have made the city a major commercial centre.

avenue for trying to correct the regional imbalance of employment opportunities in Britain. Cardiff has the Mint. Glasgow has the headquarters of the National Savings Bank. The Forestry Commission has gone to Edinburgh. Private firms are doing the same, to some extent. Barclays Bank decided to move its head office to Knutsford in Cheshire.

The imbalance in job opportunities remains. Regional rates of unemployment stubbornly refuse to conform to a national pattern. But efforts are being made to find remedies. What is perhaps most important is that people are now aware of the problem and of the need to diversify. It is hard to imagine that people in the less prosperous regions will give up their efforts to equalize job opportunities.

[1] *Industry and Empire*   E. J. Hobsbawm   (PENGUIN)
[2] Toothill Report 1961, paragraph 23:18   H.M.S.O.
[3] Article by Peter Lennox-Kerr   (THE GUARDIAN, 22 October 1973)

Attracting New Industry

'Between ourselves,' said the manager of an employment exchange in central Scotland, 'the most thriving growth industry at the moment is the promotion of industry.'[1]

The list of organizations which are trying to attract new firms, from anywhere, into Scotland is long. And the same mixture of public and private bodies can be seen actively at work in the other relatively depressed regions of the north and west of Britain.

1 The Government's Scottish Development Agency, and various branches of the Scottish Office, the Highlands and Islands Development Board, the North of Scotland Hydro-Electric Board are examples of Government bodies.

2 Business bodies like the Scottish Council (Development and Industry) and local chambers of commerce are also involved.

3 Local bodies such as the North East of Scotland Development Authority (N.E.S.D.A.), Industrial Promotion Officers employed by several local authorities, new town development corporations are also part of the army of industrial promoters.

Although their efforts have had many individual successes, the uncertainty of the employment base in many parts of the country reflects what still has to be done. When the British economy runs into difficulties, it is the 'peripheral' regions, furthest from London and the south-east, which suffer first, and which are the last to recover. When London sneezes, the north catches a cold.

PROBLEMS OF PROMOTION

The problem of attracting new industries away from the southern parts of Britain is what economists call 'immobility of capital due to locational inertia'. In plain language, it is very difficult to persuade firms to set up factories away from the 'traditional' areas for their industry.

The motor vehicle assemblers, for instance, were most reluctant to leave their West Midlands heartland in the 1960s to set up plants on Merseyside and in the west of Scotland. A survey by B. J. Loasby[2] of firms which had been persuaded to leave Birmingham (because of re-development of areas of that city) found that although about a third of the 200 firms were most reluctant to leave, only about 10 per cent regretted the move once it had been made. But the great majority went to sites as close to Birmingham as possible, in spite of encouragement to go to Development Districts further away, where they would have received financial assistance from Government, eager to attract new industry there. He found that firms had not always given thorough thought to the best site for their operations.

A (1975) survey by W. F. Lever[3] of related industries found that many groups of industries which did a lot of business with each other were very reluctant to move without their 'partner' industry or industries. He found a high degree of association between textile machinery and cotton goods, plastics materials and general chemicals, machine tools and motor vehicles, and between scientific instruments and radio and telecommunications equipment. The extent of this association between related industries is *greater* for the new industries than for the older ones.

For those promoting industrial diversification in the older industrial areas, this may be both good and bad news. It is clearly bad if it means that firms will not move away from their suppliers. But it is good if the establishment of one large firm attracts a host of component suppliers also.

External economies of scale

The problem facing all who wish to wheedle modern industries out of their existing areas is that once an industry is established in an area, for whatever reason, past or present, good or bad, the firms in that area enjoy what economists call 'external economies of scale'. Simply by being there, firms can expect savings in their costs of production. The main reasons for this are given here.

Experienced labour force

The labour force in a 'traditional' area becomes accustomed to the ways of the industry. There is a pool of skilled manpower. Technical colleges in the area will offer courses which are suitable for local trades, like metallurgy in Sheffield, marine engineering in Newcastle, furniture technology in High Wycombe. The work disciplines that industry demands are learned unconsciously by the local population. When B.M.C. went to Bathgate in the early 1960s, they found that the ex-miners of West Lothian not only did not have the skills that were necessary for work on the truck assembly line—these could mostly be learned in a short time, but also that the miners found the disciplines of working at the pace of a machine difficult to come to terms with. This meant that they had few experienced hands, and they suffered from a high turnover in the work force.

Component suppliers

In an established area, there will be a wide range of component suppliers and firms carrying out specialist services, such as repairs to machinery, transport, waste disposal. For instance, it would not be economic even for the large motor manufacturers to make their own tyres or lights or batteries. Production of these is in the hands of huge firms, like Lucas, Dunlop, Triplex, G.K.N. (Guest, Keen & Nettlefold). To avoid having to keep large stocks of the thousands of component parts that go into motor vehicles, which would be a costly business, the assemblers must be near their suppliers, who are concentrated in the West Midlands. Transport and/or storage costs must go up if the firm is far from its suppliers.

Commercial services

Related commercial services also appear in an established area. Banks get to know about the nature of the industry's business, and may be more helpful with finance because of this greater understanding. Trade associations help with industrial relations, marketing, technical advice and advertising. Distance from these would reduce the level of personal contact, and most business people feel that personal contact is most important.

Process specialization

In the cotton towns of north-east Lancashire, there has always been a high degree of specialization. Although many of these firms are now co-ordinated within large groups, the pattern of process specialization continues. Bolton, Oldham and Rochdale are spinning towns; the yarn they produce is woven in Burnley, Blackburn or Accrington, and it may be finished in Manchester, where it is sold. Managements can concentrate on one process at which their expertise should build up. The same is true of a firm with several plants in the same area, each one concentrating on one or a number of related tasks in the total productive process.

The savings which a firm makes by producing in an area which is traditional for its industry are an important factor in choosing a location for a new plant. An area which is keen to attract the firm will have to demonstrate categorically that it can offer manufacturing costs so much lower as to compensate for the advantages lost by leaving the traditional area.

INFLUENCES ON LOCATION

Psychological influences

Many people feel, not least those whose job is industrial promotion, that businessmen are very conservative in respect of chosen locations. They become attached to established areas for other than economic motives. Provided they can prove a case to inquisitive shareholders their first choice is to stay where they are. The Loasby survey mentioned above bears this out.

The reputation of an area may have a negative effect. The visual evidence of industrial dereliction, grime and vast monotonous areas of crumbling back-to-back or tenement housing may deter the executives who must accompany the firm. They may be predisposed to find fault with the area so as to avoid the horrors which they fear may lie in store. Many argue that these factors are of considerable importance. This batch of psychological influences on the choice of location is sometimes half-jokingly referred to as the 'theory of the chairman's wife'. The implication is that if the company chairman's wife likes the area, the company will give its claims due consideration. If its reputation or the quality of life there do not appeal to that lady, the company will be reluctant to submit to the attractions of the area.

Transport

How far these psychological motives operate, on a conscious or unconscious level, to determine industrial location cannot be stated without dispute. The economic influences are much clearer. They are based on production costs. The firm will settle in an area which offers the lowest costs of production.

It is important to emphasize that 'production costs' includes *all* costs involved and not just manufacturing costs. In other words, transport costs are included. In fact, transport costs have a considerable importance as far as firms themselves are concerned.

Transport costs and peripheral regions

This acts against those regions which are on the periphery of the country. In a 1974 report, *Economic Development and Devolution*, the Scottish Council Research Institute emphasized the disadvantages of Scotland's peripheral position. For most industries, a site in Scotland adds to their costs. The estimates vary from an extra 1 per cent (Toothill Report 1961) to 4 per cent (in a survey in the food processing industry).

Transport needs

1 Raw materials In an industry where raw materials are bulky, and in one where they are numerous, like the motor vehicle assembly industry, savings can be made by choosing a site as near to the supply of these components or raw materials as possible. The prime sites for steel mills are now at the coast. In their 1972 development plan, the British Steel Corporation chose three coastal sites for the construction of new, large-scale steel-making plants—at Redcar on Teesside, at Scunthorpe on Humberside and at Port Talbot in south Wales—since the bulk of Britain's iron ore, which is one of the basic elements in steel-making, and a great deal of scrap iron, which is another important element, are imported from abroad.

For handling bulk imported cargoes, specialized facilities are clearly important. A great deal of money has been put into developing the ports in relatively depressed regions, to encourage firms to move.

2 Markets In industries where the final product is bulky, like beer, savings will be possible by locating close to the customers. This is the case with much of the steel industry. The various steel-making areas tend to specialize in products which are most used by nearby industry. Sheffield produces much of the sheet steel for the Midlands car industry. The west of Scotland has long specialized in heavy plates and shipbuilding and industrial plant.

The same holds true where the product of the industry is very small and aimed at the consumer. In the domestic electrical goods industry a very large number of relatively small consignments must be sent out, to wholesalers or directly to retail outlets. Locating near the biggest market, where large numbers of relatively affluent people live, will cut down the total transport bill.

Improvements in transport

The most affluent markets are still very firmly in the southern part of Britain. The relatively depressed regions of the country must improve transportation facilities so as to reduce their clear disadvantages here. The freight-liner service (moving containers by rail) and the electrification of the main west coast rail route from

Ports—are there facilities for handling exports or imports? This is Grangemouth's container terminal.

London to Manchester/Liverpool and then to Glasgow are British Rail's efforts to speed up and reduce the unit cost of transportation from the northern regions to the mass markets of the south. The motorway system, such as the extension of the M1 to Yorkshire, the M62 linking Lancashire to the port of Hull (eventually), the M74 and M6 in Scotland and the north-west, and the M8 spanning central Scotland, and a host of improvements to existing roads are meant to speed up road transport links, especially to the ports.

Greenock (Clydeport), Liverpool (Seaforth Docks) and Humberside (Immingham) are equipped to handle containers for export.

Movement of personnel is an important factor. Salesmen must be able to reach clients rapidly, wherever they are. It is undoubtedly less easy to service potential customers from an isolated location than from the south-east with its regular air and rail services. Dundee has campaigned for many years for a regular air service to persuade interested industrialists that they would not be out of touch if they settled there. Telephone, telex and other information-transfer services are also important. The extension of subscriber-trunk-dialling (S.T.D.) to Europe and North America is an urgent priority as far as the relatively depressed regions are concerned.

Transport costs and the businessman

Although transport figures highly in businessmen's assessment of ideal location, more objective analysis (by the economist Sargent Florence) has shown that for most industries, transport costs are not a significant factor, within reason, in choosing from a number of locations.

But, so long as industrialists *think* that transport is important, it will continue to affect those areas which are distant from the mass markets and communications centres of the southern part of Britain. Many feel, in fact, that European economic integration will further jeopardize the chances of those areas, including all six of Britain's relatively depressed regions, which are outside the so-called 'golden triangle'. This is a name given to the area of northern France, western West Germany, Belgium, Luxembourg, the Netherlands and south-east England where a very large proportion of the Community's most affluent people live. It is argued that more than ever, industries will feel that they must locate in the south-east to be within close range of this golden triangle of the Common Market.

Land

The availability of land may be of some importance. To a small firm, a ready-built factory, especially if there is reduced initial rent, as in Government advance factories, will perhaps be attractive. Although there are pronounced local variations in land prices and building costs, these constitute a very small part of total production costs. The offer of a properly serviced site, with water,

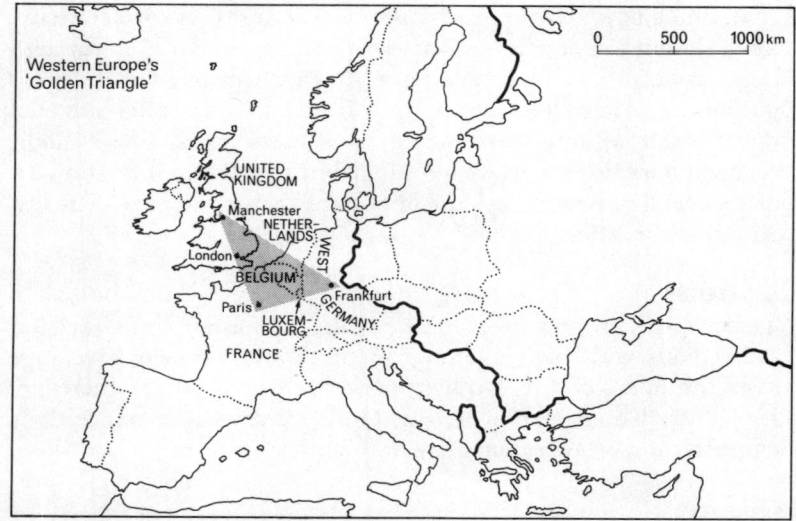

In the small triangle formed by Frankfurt–Paris–Manchester, 40 per cent of the spending power of western Europe is concentrated.

sewage disposal pipes, electricity and so on laid on, on an industrial estate, whether privately run, managed by a local authority or by a Government body (the English/Scottish/Welsh Industrial Estates Corporation), may help to attract a firm.

Finance

Although rates of interest on borrowed money vary hardly at all throughout Britain, there may be some variation as to availability. Firms may have generous credit facilities in an area where they are well established. Moving to a location in a relatively depressed region, or anywhere else for that matter, may mean that they lose this 'trusted customer' status at the bank. Several schemes have been tried, by local authorities, banks and other bodies, to provide attractive credit facilities to firms who settle in one of the poorer areas of the country.

Power supply

At one time, power supplies were vitally important in determining the choice of site. When coal provided all industrial muscle, its bulk made it wise to locate near to a supply of it. With electricity being available throughout the country by means of the national grid, this is nowadays of little importance. Large users of electricity, like aluminium-smelters, can gain some advantage through negotiation of concessionary rates, as with the smelter at Invergordon in Easter Ross. Oil users will find that a coastal site cuts down costs. Large-scale water consumers might find slight regional variations worth exploiting. But the availability and cost of power is not nowadays an important factor for most firms in choosing a location.

Labour

The availability and cost of labour are important. Superficially, the regions with high unemployment should have an advantage over the areas of the southern part of Britain where there are frequently labour shortages. But there are several considerations of greater importance than mere numbers.

Quality

Firstly, the labour must be of the right sort. Some 60 to 70 per cent of Scotland's many unemployed have no particular skill. This will not suit many of the new, science-based firms, such as electronics. They may have to 'poach' skilled manpower away from existing firms with higher wages, thus losing any advantage that may exist due to slightly lower wage rates. Or they will have to set up costly training programmes.

Reliability

Secondly, the labour relations record will indicate the reliability of the labour force. In 1972, Scotland had 9 per cent of all the U.K.s employees. But Scotland accounted for 17·1 per cent of all the days lost through strike action—nearly twice its 'fair share'. This has been a consistent pattern since the war; and it is generally true of other, older industrial areas. Their legacy from the past is as much distrust between man and boss as environmental pollution. It is sometimes said that tensions are severe in contracting industries, and this explains the situation, since it is clear that the older industrial areas have more than their fair share of such contracting industries. But Scotland, with only 4 per cent of jobs in the U.K. motor vehicle industry, accounted for no less than 22 per cent of all days lost in the U.K. through strikes in that industry in 1972.

The number of days lost through illness, including absenteeism, also indicates the reliability of labour to an industrialist. In a 1970/71 survey, all the relatively depressed regions showed up worse than all the better-off regions.

Region	No. of days lost
Scotland	19·9
Wales	31·2
Northern Ireland	25·0
England:	
North	23·9
North-west	20·6
Yorkshire and Humberside	20·5
East Midlands	15·1
West Midlands	14·0
South-west	15·9
East Anglia	11·3
South-east	10·4

Table 5.1   *Number of days absence (certified by a doctor) per worker (1970–71) in U.K. regions.*

Undoubtedly, the air of depression that accompanies life in many areas of Britain has much to do with this sad state. But the industrialist will see it as no part of his obligations to improve the morale and thus the health of a depressed area.

Costs

But by far the most important factor is labour costs. In fact, if a relatively depressed region is to winkle a firm out of the economic and psychological security of its established area, it is largely on the assessment of labour costs that they will succeed or fail.

There are two elements to labour costs. The first is the wage that is paid; the second is the productivity of labour—how many units of output an average workman produces in an hour or week or year.

Wage-rate differentials

If the going wage rate in its existing area is £50 per week, a firm may be attracted to an area where the rate is only £40 a week. The experienced and reliable work force in their existing plant produce 100 units on average per week. The labour cost of each unit of output is this one-hundredth of £50 = 50p. The inexperienced work force in the low wage area, however, can turn out only 75 units on average per week. The labour cost of each unit of output is 53·3p. The firm will stay where it is—other things being equal.

In fact, wage differentials in Britain are not wide. National negotiation of basic wage rates ensures that there is little difference within an industry between regions. Greater overtime, and productivity bonuses in some areas bring about a divergence, but it is very small in Britain compared to other industrialized countries. Average earnings in Scotland are about 2·5 to 3 per cent lower than the U.K. average; but basic wage rates vary less than that. Thus, for reputable firms of any size, there is little future in exploiting regional wage differentials.

Productivity

Productivity varies much more. There are such enormous variations between particular concerns in a region, however, that it is really rather unfair to compare regions as a whole. But industrialists do. And they find that productivity in general in the relatively depressed regions falls behind the national average. Nor is this situation being remedied. Between 1958 and 1968, productivity in U.K. industry rose by 48 per cent. During the same period, productivity in Scottish industry rose by 43 per cent.

It is essential to overcome this difference if profit-seeking firms are to be attracted into areas like Scotland which need them. What is the cause of Scotland's poor productivity record?

1   One cause is the *bad labour relations* situation already mentioned. Friction and distrust, which the bad strike figures imply, are not conducive to boosting productivity. There is widespread over-manning in Scotland in comparison with other areas, in some industries anyway, such as steel.

2   The *smaller scale* of the average firm's operations in Scotland means that firms are not able to exploit fully the savings that come from large production runs.

3   In some cases, firms that have come to Scotland have either left *suppliers* behind, in which case they have experienced delays which show up adversely in productivity figures. Or they have tried to be their own suppliers, in which case they produce the sort of poor productivity which so often results from tackling too wide a range of jobs rather than specializing.

4   There is little doubt that, with wide exceptions, the average Scottish worker has less 'power to his elbow' in the form of *tools*

and machines than the average U.K. worker. This situation is changing, thanks to an influx of American money and the success of Government schemes to encourage the installation of more capital equipment. Scotland in the late 1960s and 1970s has been getting slightly more than the 9 per cent of U.K. investment in tools and machinery to which the size of its work force would entitle it.

5   Poor quality of *management* is often attributed to Scotland. This is explained in many ways, from 'defects' in the national character, which does not value initiative in business, to the attraction of the best talent away to more rewarding areas.

6   The smaller scale of the average Scottish firm and the growth of a *branch-plant economy* in Scotland has proved unattractive to many ambitious managers. The implications of the branch-plant economy are particularly serious.

A survey was conducted (by W. F. Luttrell[4]) into firms who set up a new factory away from their existing area of operations. He found that where the plant was of an economic size, its cost, reflecting its levels of productivity, compared favourably with the 'parent' plant(s) in the old area (after a settling-in period), *provided* the plant had a fair measure of independence. Where a plant was set up as a 'branch' of the main factory, where many decisions had to be referred to this 'parent' factory, costs were markedly higher, reflecting lower productivity.

With many honourable exceptions, firms which have been tempted to Scotland, perhaps because of financial inducements from the Government, have tended to set up branch factories. They have been seen as additional to their main concern further south. Orders may have been allocated on the basis that the branch plant takes the orders that the main plant cannot handle. This has meant fluctuations in the level of work, and periods when machinery and people have been idle. This shows up in poor productivity figures.

What is more, when there has been a recession in orders, the Scottish plant has been the first to be cut back severely, putting people out of work. This was seen in 1973 when an interruption to the steady onward progress of the U.K. electronics industry caused widespread lay-offs in Scotland. Only 8 per cent of the electronics industry in Scotland is Scottish-owned. The rest is owned by outside firms who often operate their Scottish concerns as 'branches' of their main business—although some, such as Ferranti, do confer a high degree of independence.

This situation typifies the vicious circle in which areas like Scotland find themselves. Firms are reluctant to risk setting up an independent concern in an area with traditionally low productivity. If they do set up a plant, they keep it under tight control. When a cutback in orders comes, the branch plant is cut back first. This guarantees poor productivity figures, which confirms the firm in their policy of keeping detailed control over their branch plant operations. They will tend to starve it of further finance which denies it the chance to make technical advances which an independent management might introduce. The real sufferers, of course, are the people whose jobs are insecure as a result.

The problems which face a relatively depressed region in a free enterprise economy seem daunting. It is not to be wondered at that they have cried out for Government help.

---

[1] 'Scotch Broth' by Jane Morton   (NEW SOCIETY, 27 July 1972)
[2] 'Making Location Policy Work' by B. J. Loasby   (LLOYD'S BANK REVIEW, January 1967)
[3] *Regional Studies*, Vol 6 No 4 by W. F. Lever
[4] *Factory Location and Industrial Movement*   W. F. Luttrell   (NATIONAL INSTITUTE OF ECONOMIC RESEARCH)

The Rôle of Government

Governments' rôle in industrial change has been growing rapidly in the 1960s and 1970s. A pre-war observer of laissez-faire inaction would be truly amazed. Government action in respect of industry can be viewed under two headings—Government policies which have encouraged industrial change, and Government policies to alleviate the hardships brought about by industrial change.

GOVERNMENT POLICIES

On industrial development

Help towards industrial development has been overwhelmingly piece-meal. Before the 1975 Industry Act, there were few co-ordinated policies for industry as a whole. For individual industries, there have been myriad measures to help effect what was seen at the time as progress. Cotton, shipbuilding, electronics (especially computers) and the whole field of electrical engineering (G.E.C.–A.E.I.–E.E. merger of 1968), motor vehicles, machine tools, aircraft, coal, steel—these are just some of the many industries whose progress has been the object of Government attention, whether they wished it or not. In some cases, Government has assumed direct responsibility for an industry through nationalization, as with shipbuilding, aircraft, coal and steel from the above list.

Such general measures as have been tried have been limited in their scope and in their consequent ability to stimulate controlled and co-ordinated industrial 'progress'. These general stimulants include the following:

1 Taxation The introduction of Corporation Tax in 1965 (and its reform in the early 1970s) was meant to stimulate industrial

investment by encouraging retention of company profits. The Selective Employment Tax of 1966 (abolished 1973) was a payroll tax meant to shift employment from (non-exporting) services to (export-oriented) manufacturing industry. Depreciation allowances, introduced for manufacturing industry in general in 1972, allow spending on capital equipment to be deducted from taxable profits.

2 Competition One aim of the operation of the Monopolies and Mergers Commission (first set up in 1948) has been to prevent over-large firms from ignoring progress while they sit back and take advantage of the lack of competition.

3 Structure In some cases, larger units are deemed desirable to facilitate the onward march of technical progress. The work of the Industrial Reorganization Corporation (I.R.C.) in the late 1960s was aimed at the merger of firms to create just such large units (as with the G.E.C.–A.E.I.–E.E. merger in 1968 cited above).

4 Training The Industrial Training Act of 1964 which set up twenty-seven Industrial Training Boards and the expansion of the work of the Government's Training Services Agency are aimed at ensuring that the 'human element' in industrial progress is given due attention.

5 Research and development The steady work of the Government research establishments, the sponsorship of research by the publicly funded research councils, the financial backing of such individual projects as Concorde or the (abandoned) hovertrain are part of the Government's endeavours to boost Britain's economic growth.

6 Planning The National Economic Development Council (Neddy) was created in 1962 to try to establish broad economic objectives, to examine obstacles to industrial growth and to discuss their removal. The National Plan of 1965 was an attempt to convert this work from the 'notional' to the 'practical'. Significantly, this ambitious strategy failed utterly.

The Industry Act of 1975 claimed that it was the first co-ordinated attempt at *The Regeneration of British Industry* (as the white paper introducing it was entitled). It aimed, through the National Enterprise Board (N.E.B.), to make use of public funds to stimulate industrial progress. The N.E.B. was designed to be flexible in its approach and comprehensive in its coverage. It can lend; it can hold shares in and even buy out firms. The N.E.B.

is a state holding company on the lines of Italy's and Sweden's successful examples of publicly-inspired industrial development. Planning agreements between the Government and individual firms, to stimulate the development of firms with public financial assistance, were another of the Act's measures. But to what extent co-ordination of industrial development can be achieved in a basically free enterprise economy remains to be seen.

On the consequences of industrial change

In Chapter 3, four major consequences of industrial change were indicated. Government policy, through the work of the Training Services Agency of the Manpower Services Commission and the twenty-seven Industrial Training Boards, has aimed to provide for the new skills that are needed as industrial techniques change.

On changed working conditions, little Government action has been taken beyond the stage of research, such as that of the Work Research Unit of the Department of Employment. The disclosure of company information to work-people (required by the 1975 Industry Act) and proposals for greater industrial democracy, whereby working people might become more involved in the firms for which they work, are stumbling attempts to seek possible solutions, or palliatives as cynics would claim.

In contrast, Government policy with respect to those regions which have been left behind in the transformation of the British economy has become an important political issue. Though large sums are now devoted to incentives to attract private firms to settle in relatively depressed regions, the case for Government intervention in this field is by no means universally accepted.

CASE FOR INTERVENTION

The case for Government intervention to try to rectify the uneven distribution of industrial opportunities rests on several bases.

Unemployment and poor living conditions
in older industrial areas

Not the least important is the concentration of technically progressive, expanding industries in the Midlands and south-east of England while declining traditional industries remain concentrated in the coalfield areas to the north and west of Britain, where people still want to live. Efforts that have been made to move firms in these modern industries have met with limited success. Firms have been prepared to move to new sites, but within the same region.

The environmental, and human, dereliction which the nineteenth century has left in the older industrial areas of the north and west needs considerable finance to remedy. This is difficult in areas where earning power is impaired by high unemployment.

Political motives

People who live in areas where unemployment is endemic, and where prospects for themselves and for their children are bleak, might be expected to turn to the Government for help. It has become a political issue. Those areas of the country which suffer particularly from relatively high unemployment tend disproportionately to support the Labour party.

Area	%
Great Britain	49·5
Scotland	52·7
North England	57·1
North-west England	52·1
Yorkshire and Humberside	56·6
Wales	64·4
South-east England	47·5
East Anglia	42·8

The share of the overall vote in Great Britain (in constituencies where the parties put up candidates) was:

Labour	38·0%	Liberal	23·6%
Conservative	38·8%	Other	8·5%

Table 6.1 *Labour party's percentage share of votes cast for the Labour and Conservative parties (only) in the General Election, February 1974*

It was as a result of its ascendancy in the relatively depressed northern and western regions of Britain that the Labour party scraped to power after the closely-fought general election of February 1974. Their 37·9 per cent share of the two main parties' joint vote in the affluent south-east outside Greater London contrasts with a 60 per cent or higher share of this joint vote in industrially depressed areas like Clydeside, Tyneside and south Wales.

The Labour party has much to lose by taking no action to remedy the sad economic state of much of these depressed regions, especially in Scotland and Wales where nationalist parties have been applying increasing pressure since the late 1960s.

The Labour party is more prepared to intervene in the economy to achieve social goals; and its egalitarian tradition makes it inevitable that it is more committed to regional redistribution of economic opportunities than its Conservative opponents.

The Conservatives have an antipathy to supporting 'lame duck' concerns (industries which cannot survive market disciplines), which makes them less inclined to become involved. Since they have fewer votes in the north and west, they have less to lose.

Congestion in expanding areas

Congestion in the newer industrial areas is giving concern. Long and expensive journeys to work, high cost housing due to fierce competition for land and houses impair the quality of life for many people. The costs of operating in a congested area are growing. Wages must be high to compensate for high transport costs in getting to work and because of the need to attract labour away from the many alternative employments. Warehousing and space of all sorts is expensive. Much of the land in the southern part of Britain is good farming land. Continued industrial expansion reduces the area that is available for producing food.

Pressure on resources in areas of expansion may lead to inflation, which will affect the country adversely in many ways.

Waste

The most basic argument is that it is wasteful to leave unemployed resources in some areas when there is widespread demand for economic growth.

CASE AGAINST INTERVENTION

The argument for Government intervention in location of industries is by no means universally accepted. Many people feel that 'businessmen know best' and that they should be left to choose the site where they can produce at lowest cost. Others acknowledge that businessmen do not, as Loasby's survey indicated, always choose the best site. But they argue that if industrialists are confident about their choice they will back it up more efficiently than if a Government department makes the decision for them.

Loss of external economies of scale
and falling productivity

If a firm is induced away from an established area for its industry, it will lose the 'external economies of scale' which it derives from producing in an area of component suppliers and specialists. Productivity will suffer. Costs will rise. British manufacturers' prices may be pushed up, or profits will be cut, reducing the funds available for installing new machinery to take advantage of technical advances. Higher prices will damage export potential; imports may rise as cheaper foreign products are preferred to increasingly costly home-produced commodities.

Far from promoting growth, sending firms to areas where low productivity will result would hold back the overall level of national production.

Push v. Pull

These gloomy analyses carry much weight with the business community and many economists. They argue for a policy of encouraging the workers to migrate to where they find work, as so many have done already. By this method, production will be concentrated in those areas where productivity is highest, so boosting the rate of national economic growth. This is sometimes called a 'pull' policy. The idea of 'leading workers to the work' is certainly favoured by those who are alarmed at the growth in public spending to prop up ailing industries.

The 'push' policy, based on the idea of 'taking work to the workers', has been intermittently applied in Britain since the war. The policy before the war was largely of the 'pull' variety, aimed at offering opportunities for those who left the areas of highest unemployment in the north and west.

REGIONAL DEVELOPMENT POLICIES

Pre-war measures

The 1934 Special Areas Act was the first, lukewarm venture into help for the depressed areas. It applied only to areas which were 'special' because of the hideous level of unemployment there. Commissioners were appointed to spend the pitifully small sum of £2 million a year to make the Special Areas—south Wales, central Scotland, the west Cumberland coast and the north-east coast of

England—more attractive for incoming industry. Further legislation in 1936 and 1937 extended the scheme modestly and allowed the establishment of industrial estates, on which sites were to be offered to expanding firms at low rents.

It was clear that these measures were painfully inadequate. The Barlow Report, published in 1940, came out strongly for much greater Government intervention in favour of depressed areas, and it recommended that Government should actually restrict further expansion in London and other prosperous areas.

The immediate post-war years

The Labour Government of 1945–51 was responsible for two developments. The 1945 Distribution of Industry Act provided for loans to firms moving into the Development Areas (the renamed Special Areas, whose number was gradually increased). It also gave the Government powers to acquire land and build 'advance factories' (on industrial estates or elsewhere) to offer to incoming firms, at reduced rents. The 1947 Town and Country Planning Act introduced the only direct control which Government has ever had over the location of industry—the Industrial Development Certificate (I.D.C.). A firm needed an I.D.C. from the Government before it could build a factory of any size (now over 465 square metres). By this method, it was intended to restrict the growth of factories in the prosperous areas and divert them to the Development Areas.

The 1950s

Increasing concern with balancing the international payments by encouraging all-out economic growth and exports diverted Government attention from redistribution of industry. The Development Areas' share of new factory space fell from 50 per cent in 1948 to 18 per cent in 1950. Public opinion tolerated this because of generally low rates of unemployment until the late 1950s.

The growth of international competition, with the re-establishment of the shattered economies of continental Europe and Japan, led to a rise in unemployment in 1957–58, with much higher rates in the older industrial areas, especially in the southeast Lancashire cotton industry and the shipbuilding industry on the Clyde and the Tyne.

Measures from 1958–64

Finance was made available to expanding firms in areas of high unemployment by the 1958 Distribution of Industry Act. But continuing disparities between regions with respect to unemployment brought about the 1960 Local Employment Act. It was at the same time more helpful to areas with high levels of unemployment, and less ambitious to encourage a more even distribution of industrial opportunities. 165 Development Districts, where the rate of unemployment was 4·5 per cent or more, replaced the large Development Areas. More generous finance than before was available for buildings, plant and machinery, and for working capital to firms expanding in the Development Districts. A further Act of 1963 introduced standard grants of 10 per cent of the cost of plant and machinery and 25 per cent of the cost of industrial buildings, to relieve uncertainties for firms planning to set up in the Development Districts.

Growth area approach

This concentration on 'pockets' of high unemployment was much criticized. A region-wide approach to diversifying industry was favoured by most expert opinion. Within the older industrial areas which had few attractions for new firms, there were centres which had distinct economic advantages, such as new towns, coastal sites and places close to road/rail connections. Public spending on the infrastructure of roads and other transport facilities, training and other business requirements should be concentrated in these potential growth areas. The new firms attracted would have spillover benefits for the surrounding, older areas.

Regional planning councils

The 1964–70 Labour Government set up advisory councils in each of the eight regions of England and in Scotland and Wales to advise Government how best to spend public money to improve each region's infrastructure and to identify growth areas.

Grants and incentives 1966–70

In 1966 the Industrial Development Act brought about considerable changes in the support given by Government to firms going to the relatively depressed regions. Development Areas—covering most of Scotland and Wales, the north-east of England, Mersey-side, parts of Devon and Cornwall—replaced the Development Districts. Grants were made available on a more generous scale for firms installing plant and machinery in these Areas. 40 per cent of spending on plant (45 per cent for the first two years) and 25 per cent of spending on industrial buildings could be reclaimed from the Government. Assistance was also given for industrial training, for clearing derelict land and for projects in areas of especially high unemployment. From 1967, a Regional Employment Premium (R.E.P.) of £1.50 a week for each employee was payable to industrial firms, though not in the service industries, in the Development Areas, to encourage labour-using firms to set up there. Government was spending over £250 million a year on encouraging firms to expand in the Development Areas. Following the Hunt Report in 1969, the Government extended some of the cash and other benefits to 'intermediate' or 'grey' areas of Lancashire, Yorkshire and north Derbyshire which suffered, to a lesser degree, from the same problems of industrial imbalance as the Development Areas.

Changing Conservative policy 1970–74

The 1970 Conservative Government was more conscious of the defects of unselective cash grants than of their benefits—200–250,000 extra jobs in the period 1963–70. They argued that Development Areas wanted *profitable* firms. Government aid should encourage only profitable firms, not *all* firms. A system of tax allowances was devised whereby expenditure on plant and machinery could be deducted from profits before they were taxed. Thus only profitable firms would get the advantages.

In 1971, the Government re-introduced cash grants in Special Development Districts—areas of high unemployment. A comment on the lack of success of regional development policies is that these areas were almost identical to the Special Areas of 1934. The Industry Act of 1972 brought back cash grants for three categories of Assisted Areas.

Special Development Areas were the Special Development Districts of 1971—the areas with the most urgent need for more jobs. With the re-constituted Development Areas, they covered much the same area as the pre-1970 Development Areas. The Intermediate Areas covered areas similar to those identified in

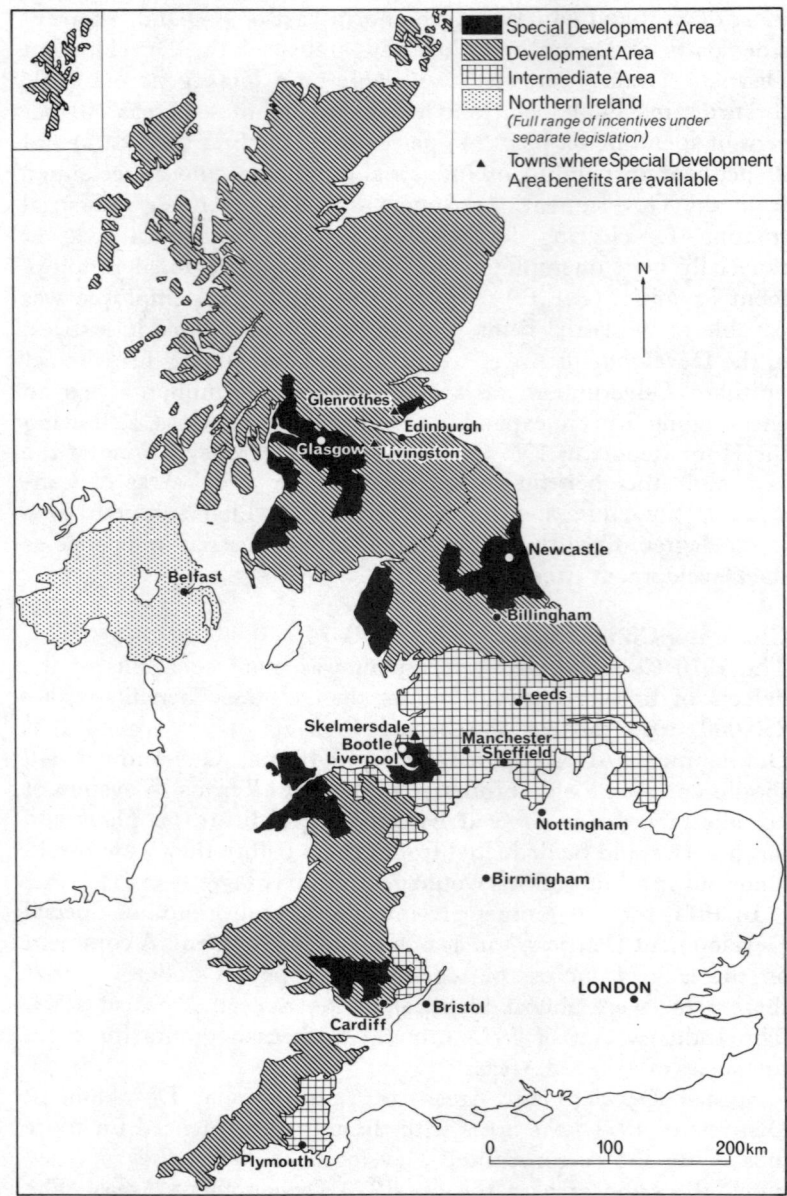

The Assisted Areas of Britain (1976).

the 1969 Hunt Report. The areas covered are shown on the map opposite. The scale of financial assistance can be seen in Table 6.2.

	New machinery, plant and mining works (%)	Building and non-mining works (%)
Special Development Areas	22	22
Development Areas	20	20
Intermediate Areas	nil	20

Table 6.2   *Investment Grants under the Industry Act of 1972*

The cost of this programme of regional development grants was about £225 million in 1974–75.

In addition to the standard grants, Government could help, with loans, any project in the Assisted Areas to improve employment prospects. They could also pay for the removal of machinery from an old site to a new site in an Assisted Area, and could contribute to redundancy payments paid to workers by a firm moving from an old site to one in an Assisted Area.

The mid-1970s
Thus, by the mid-1970s, Government assistance for regional development had three arms:

1   direct controls over building—such as industrial Development Certificates (I.D.C.s) dating from 1947, but seldom used to direct industry;

2   inducements—such as grants for equipment and buildings (from 1972); Regional Employment Premium (R.E.P.) (1967–77); training grants (from 1966); advance factories (from 1945);

3   developing the infrastructure—of roads, ports, housing, technical training and other business requirements in relatively depressed regions.

The Common Market and the Development Areas
In 1973, the E.E.C. announced the establishment of a Regional Development Fund. The original plan for a three-year programme to inject about £1000 million into the Community's poorest regions, including all of Britain's Assisted Areas, met with objections. A new and less ambitious scheme was finally launched in 1975, with powers to spend £541·7 million (1300 million units of account) over 1975, 1976 and 1977. Britain's share was set at

28 per cent, which is greater than its 15 per cent share of the contributions to the Fund.

Grants are also given by the Social Fund of the E.E.C. for training, such as £2,100,000 in 1974 to the Training Services Agency for training instructors, young people who cannot find work and redundant older workers in Britain's Assisted Areas. The European Coal and Steel Community is empowered to give grants to ease problems arising from adjustments within the coal or steel industries, like the grant of £10·44 million in 1975 to 11,921 ex-miners made redundant by twenty-seven pit closures (mostly in Scotland and the north-east of England) during 1973 and 1974. The European Investment Bank looks with favour on projects to improve the infrastructure of backward regions.

Criticisms

There are many who feel that policies for regional development have failed utterly. A 1974 House of Commons report described the post-war experience thus:

> much has been spent, and much may well have been wasted. Regional policy has been . . . a game of hit and miss, played with more enthusiasm than success.[1]

The report criticized 'blanket' investment grants which go to all firms, regardless. It pointed out that some firms, like the oil exploration industry, would have *paid* to be allowed to settle in eastern Scotland; yet they could claim grants like any other firm setting up in an Assisted Area. Other concerns may have needed much greater assistance, which would have paid off eventually.

A large group holds the opinion that the best deal for the depressed regions is to concentrate investment in the most productive areas of business to produce the biggest possible national drive towards growth. They claim that it is better to be relatively 'backward' in a rich country than 'equal' in a poor one.

ECONOMIC POLICY AND INDUSTRY

Certainly, regional development policy is only one part of the Government's total economic strategy. Government now intervenes in the workings of the economy to an extent that is unprece-

| GRANTS up to 22% of expenditure on all capital projects | REGIONAL EMPLOYMENT PREMIUM[1] £2 per adult employed in manufacturing industry |

GRANTS
up to 22% of expenditure on all capital projects

REGIONAL EMPLOYMENT PREMIUM[1]
£2 per adult employed in manufacturing industry

SELECTIVE FINANCIAL ASSISTANCE
for projects to create or maintain employment
—cheap loans;
   interest relief;
   up to 80% removal grants
—joint projects between
   private firms and N.E.B.
   or Scottish Development
   Agency

ADVANCE FACTORIES
for sale or rent—with up to 5 years rent-free

PLANNING PERMISSION
no I.D.C. needed in the Development Areas, as in other areas

LABOUR MOBILITY
helped by training grants;
up to £600 per worker transferred into a Development Area after re-training;
free fares/lodging allowances for workers transferred into Development Areas with their firms

CONTRACT PREFERENCE
may be given to firms in Development Areas bidding for government contracts

[1] Suspended from early 1977 in favour of more selective assistance.

E.E.C.
loans on favourable terms or grants from the European Investment Bank, E.C.S.C., European Social Fund, European Regional Development Fund

Incentives to expand in the Development Areas and Special Development Areas.

dented in history. Demands to curb the grosser inequalities inherent in a free enterprise economy have brought governments firmly into the economic arena.

Many industries were nationalized in the late 1940s, and steel in 1967. Controls over private firms have been steadily tightened. Growing concentrations of economic power, though often promoting economic efficiency, have alarmed many. Governments have been exercising increasing supervision over the activities of large companies. Distrust of multi-national corporations—firms operating in many countries, like Ford, Shell, Esso or Philips— is building up because of their ability to switch the emphasis of their operations from one country to another without regard to the effect on local populations, as the U.S. car giant, Chrysler, did in Europe in the mid-1970s. This will guarantee that vigilance is maintained, even stepped-up.

There have been growing demands also from industry's work force for a greater say in the vital decisions which so intimately affect their lives. Sometimes this has burst dramatically into the headlines, as with the 1971 U.C.S. work-in, or the workers' co-operatives at Kirkby (formerly Fisher-Bendix) and Meriden (motor-cycles), or the *Scottish Daily News* experiment. Usually it is a slow and steady encroachment by union negotiators on the areas formerly the sole prerogative of management. The Industry Act (1975) extended the scope for worker involvement by making company information more widely available.

Greater Government involvement is something that industry has had to get used to. Though often they have accepted this reluctantly, they have been eager also to secure Government help.

All post-war British governments have had four aims in the economic field: 1 full employment; 2 stable prices; 3 economic growth; 4 a balance of international payments.

1 To maintain full employment, governments have aimed to stimulate demand from the public for industry's wares to a level that will keep all men and machines fully occupied.

2 To ensure that prices are not pushed up by having 'too much money chasing too few goods', they have had to limit the spending power of the community.

3 To promote growth, they have boosted the level of spending so as to make it attractive for firms to install extra machines in extra factories to meet the extra demand from the public.

4   To try to boost the level of exports and cut down on imports, governments have often limited the level of spending in the domestic (British) market.

The tools that Government has to carry out these policies are basically two—*fiscal policy and monetary policy*.

With *fiscal policy*, Government can affect the amount of money in people's pockets by changing the rates of taxation. As the largest spending organization in the country, Government can greatly affect the order books of firms throughout Britain.

Monetary policy affects the ease with which people and firms can borrow money to finance purchases. The individual's hire purchase or bank loan will allow him to spend beyond his current income. Firms rely on bank loans and overdrafts for the purchase of stock.

By these methods, governments affect the level of spending that confronts British firms. Because of the divergence of methods needed for different goals—full employment requires a high level of spending, while stable prices imply restricting spending—British economic policy since 1945 has often appeared to fluctuate between 'stop' and 'go'.

This has had few beneficial effects on industry's confidence in the future. Uncertainty as to the level of the public's spending has made British industry reluctant to install machinery to exploit technical advances. This has not helped industry's efficiency and its ability to compete in a competitive world.

Britain's recurrent international problems, arising basically from a lack of competitive efficiency, have been the constant 'spanner in the works' for economic policy. Whenever Britain's economic growth performance was silencing the merchants of doom, the problems caused by the 'sucking in' of imports brought about a 'stop' situation.

Industry has had to come to terms with the uncertainty and confusion of economic policy in a confusing and uncertain world. In time-honoured British fashion, the industries which give employment to British people have muddled through. And the areas of the nineteenth-century economic revolution, left behind in the twentieth century, have muddled through also, just a little behind.

---

[1] *Regional Development Incentives*—report by the House of Commons Expenditure Committee, 1974

Further Reading

Britain: An Official Handbook (H.M.S.O.)
(prepared annually by the Reference Division of the C.O.I., it contains a general guide to the structure of industry and particular industries, and Government economic policy)

British Industries and their Organisation G. C. Allen (LONGMAN)
(historical changes in technology, markets and organization of major British industries)

Business in Britain Graham Turner (PENGUIN)
(guide to changes in and structure of the main British industries)

The Chemicals and Allied Industries Samuel Hays (HEINEMANN: Studies in the British Economy)

The Engineering Industries Samuel Hays (HEINEMANN: Studies in the British Economy)

Government Intervention and Industrial Policy A. Skuse (HEINEMANN: Studies in the British Economy)

Life in Modern Britain Peter Bromhead (LONGMAN)

Regional Planning and the Location of Industry Derek Lee (HEINEMANN: Studies in the British Economy)

Scotland: The New Future George Murray (BLACKIE)

Official Publications (H.M.S.O.):
   Abstract of Regional Statistics (annual)
   Annual Abstract of Statistics
   C.O.I. Fact Sheets on British Industry (F.S.I. series)
   Department of Employment Gazette (monthly)
   Economic Trends (monthly)
   Regional Economic Planning Councils—reports on individual regions
   Second Report of the House of Commons Expenditure Committee (1974) (on regional development incentives)
   Seventh Report of the House of Commons Expenditure Committee (1972–73) Vol. 1: Employment Services and Training
   Trade and Industry (weekly from the Department of Trade)